XERISCAPE
COLOR GUIDE

100 Water-Wise Plants for
Gardens and Landscapes

EDITED BY DAVID WINGER OF
DENVER WATER

INTRODUCTION BY KEN BALL

Published in cooperation
Denver Water and Fulcrum Publishing

USDA Zone Map

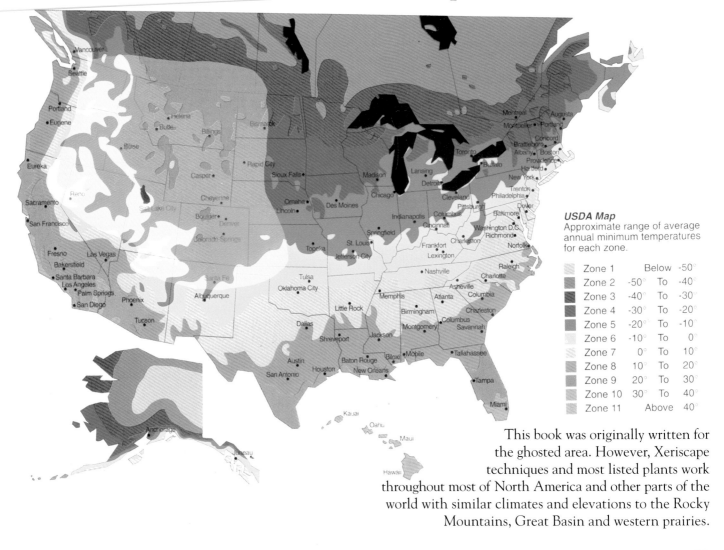

USDA Map
Approximate range of average annual minimum temperatures for each zone.

Zone 1	Below	-50°
Zone 2	-50° To	-40°
Zone 3	-40° To	-30°
Zone 4	-30° To	-20°
Zone 5	-20° To	-10°
Zone 6	-10° To	0°
Zone 7	0° To	10°
Zone 8	10° To	20°
Zone 9	20° To	30°
Zone 10	30° To	40°
Zone 11	Above	40°

This book was originally written for the ghosted area. However, Xeriscape techniques and most listed plants work throughout most of North America and other parts of the world with similar climates and elevations to the Rocky Mountains, Great Basin and western prairies.

Copyright © 1998 Denver Water

Library of Congress Cataloging-in-Publication Data

Xeriscape color guide / Denver Water.
    p.   cm.
   Companion volume to: Xeriscape plant guide. c1996.
   Includes bibliographical references and index.
   ISBN 1-55591-391-1 (pbk.)
   1. Drought tolerant plants—North America. 2. Drought tolerant plants—North America—Pictorial works. 3. Botanical illustration. 4. Xeriscaping—North America. 5. Color in gardening—North America. I. Denver (Colo.). Water Dept.
SB439.8.X47   1998
635.9'5—dc21
                    97-38109
                    CIP

Cover photograph © 1998 Charles Mann
Cover illustration © 1998 Ann Lowdermilk
Cover design by Beckie Smith

Printed by Sung In Printing Company, Seoul, Korea

0 9 8 7 6 5 4 3 2 1

Fulcrum Publishing
350 Indiana Street, Suite 350
Golden, Colorado 80401-5093 USA
(800) 992-2908 • (303) 277-1623
website: www.fulcrum-gardening.com

Acknowledgements

This book is a cooperative effort by several organizations and individuals, and most of the efforts were volunteer. Members of Xeriscape Colorado provided the overall direction to the Guide plus data from their own research and from their own gardening experience. Photographers from all over the Colorado's Front Range, Western Slope and New Mexico scoured gardens everywhere and their own files for just the right subjects. The Jefferson County Cooperative Extension horticulturist worked diligently to edit initial research. Horticulturists from Denver metropolitan garden centers, garden design businesses and Hudson Gardens, checked and double-checked for accuracy in the text, illustrations and photos. The Denver Botanic Gardens' plant illustration classes formed a special class of volunteer artists to illustrate each plant for close-up identification. The cities of Aurora, Colorado Springs, Castle Rock, Fort Morgan, Grand Junction, Greeley, Longmont, Loveland Water & Power and Platte Canyon Water & Sanitation District provided funds to make *Xeriscape Plant Guide* affordable.

It took three years, thousands of collective hours and dollars to bring this project to fruition. Denver Water and the American Water Works Association are immensely grateful to the following individuals for their hard work and support for *Xeriscape Plant Guide*.

DENVER WATER EDITOR
David Winger

ART DIRECTION & GRAPHIC DESIGN
Beckie Smith

XERISCAPE COLORADO VOLUNTEER EDITORIAL COMMITTEE
Landscape Architects and Designer:
Ken Ball • Don Godi • Tom Stephens • Marcia Tatroe

XERISCAPE COLORADO PLANT RESEARCH VOLUNTEERS
Professional and non-professional gardeners, landscape contractors, designers, architects and horticulturalists: Maryann Adams • Denise Brady • Jan Caniglia • Sara Delaloye • Connie Ellefson • Mary Ellen Keskimaki • Lisa Manke • Laura Mullen • Kathy Olsen • Donna Pacetti • Connie Rayor • Anne Sturdavant • Marcia Tatroe • Gayle Weinstein • Amy Wright • Jill Zibell

VOLUNTEER ART INSTRUCTORS AND ARTISTS
Marjorie C. Leggitt • Angela Overy • Rob Proctor

REVISING AND ORGANIZING
Judy Booton • Jane Earle • Pat Gonzales • Connie McGraw • Leslie Parker • Ethan Saunders

VOLUNTEER HORTICULTURAL REVIEW
Professional Horticulturalists: Robert Cox • Ray Daugherty • Kelly Grummons • Harriet McMillen • Bob Nold • Andrew Pierce • Marcia Tatroe • Susan Yetter

VOLUNTEER ARTISTS
Karen Boggs • Jill Buck • Cynthia Cano • Melody Durrett • Linda Evans • Susan T. Fisher • Barbara Gregg • Pamela Hoffman • Patty Homs • Sandie Howard • Jayme S. Irvin • Lynn Janicki • Allyn Jarrett • Libby Kyer • Ann Lowdermilk • Tanya McMurtry • Diana J. Neadeau/Zimmermann • Nancy Nelson • Shirley Nelson • Harriet Olds • Marie Orlin • Tana Pittman • Janice Romine • Susan Rubin • Lori Rhea Swingle • Marilyn Taylor • Debbie Brown Tejada • Linda Lorraine Wolfe

PHOTOGRAPHERS
Ken Ball • Connie Ellefson • Robert Heapes • Panayoti Kelaidis • Ed Leland • Charles Mann • Angela Overy • Kathy Olsen • Rob Proctor • Alan Rollinger • Karelle Scharff • Scott Stephens • Lori Stover • Randy Tatroe • David Winger/Denver Water.

MARKETING RESEARCH AND ANALYSIS
Steve Boand • Jon L. Farris

THANKS TO THE DENVER BOARD OF WATER COMMISSIONERS
and Denver Water's Manager Hamlet J. Barry, III for their support in the creation of this book. A special thanks to Charles G. Jordan, Denver Water's Public Affairs Director and Elizabeth Gardener, Denver Water's Water Conservation Officer for their commitment and advocacy to and for this book.

The Denver Botanic Gardens are deeply appreciated for having beautiful gardens available for our photographers and illustrators, and a wonderful library for our research. Thanks is extended to the numerous home owners and businesses who opened up their gardens to us. We are also thankful for access to the Xeriscape Demonstration Gardens located along the front range.

Illustrators

PLANT NAME: *Acer ginnala* - Amur Maple; Cynthia Cano, p.13

PLANT NAME: *Acer grandidentatum* - Bigtooth Maple; Cynthia Cano, p.14

PLANT NAME: *Aesculus glabra* - Ohio Buckeye; Cynthia Cano, p.12

PLANT NAME: *Amelanchier alnifolia* - Saskatoon Serviceberry; Marilyn Taylor, p.15

PLANT NAME: *Amorpha canescens* - Leadplant; Marilyn Taylor, p. 2

PLANT NAME: *Atriplex canescens* - Fourwing Saltbush; Lori Rhea Swingle, p. 2

PLANT NAME: *Caryopteris* x *clandonensis* - Blue Mist Spirea; Diana J. Neadeau/Zimmermann, p. 2

PLANT NAME: *Catalpa speciosa* - Western Catalpa; Ann Lowdermilk, p. 9

PLANT NAME: *Celtis occidentalis* - Hackberry; Jayme Irwin, p. 9

PLANT NAME: *Ceratoides lanata* - Winterfat; Tana Pittman, p. 3

PLANT NAME: *Cercocarpus ledifolius* - Curl-leaf Mountain Mahogany; Diana J. Neadeau/Zimmermann, p. 3

PLANT NAME: *Chamaebatiaria millefolium* - Fernbush; Susan Fisher, p. 3

PLANT NAME: *Chrysothamnus nauseosus* - Rubber Rabbitbrush; Jill Sanders Buck, p. 4

PLANT NAME: *Cotoneaster divaricatus* - Spreading Cotoneaster; Linda Lorraine Wolfe, p. 15

PLANT NAME: *Cowania mexicana* - Cliffrose; Melody Durrett, p. 4

PLANT NAME: *Crataegus crus-galli* - Cockspur Hawthorn; Allyn Jarrett, p. 12

PLANT NAME: *Fallugia paradoxa* - Apache Plume; Nancy Nelson, p. 5

PLANT NAME: *Forestiera neomexicana* - New Mexican Privet; Melody Durrett, p. 9

PLANT NAME: *Fraxinus pennsylvanica* - Green Ash; Melody Durrett, p. 10

PLANT NAME: *Gymnocladus dioica* - Kentucky Coffee Tree; Nancy Nelson, p. 10

PLANT NAME: *Hippophae rhamnoides* - Sea Buckthorn; Susan Fisher, p. 5

PLANT NAME: *Juniperus horizontalis* - Creeping Juniper; Lori Rhea Swingle, p. 5

PLANT NAME: *Juniperus scopulorum* - Rocky Mtn. Juniper; Lori Rhea Swingle, p. 6

PLANT NAME: *Cytisus scoparius* 'Moonlight' - Moonlight Broom; Pamela Hoffman, p. 4

PLANT NAME: *Kolkwitzia amabilis* - Beauty Bush; Rob Proctor, p. 6

PLANT NAME: *Koelreuteria paniculata* - Goldenrain Tree; Sandie Howard, p. 10

PLANT NAME: *Philadephus microphyllus* - Littleleaf Mockorange; Janice Romine, p. 56

PLANT NAME: *Pinus aristata* - Bristlecone Pine; Marie Orlin, p. 6

PLANT NAME: *Pinus ponderosa* - Ponderosa Pine; Marie Orlin, p. 7

PLANT NAME: *Potentilla fruticosa* - Potentilla; Ann Lowdermilk, p. 7

PLANT NAME: *Prunus armeniaca* - Apricot; Susan Fisher, p. 11

PLANT NAME: *Prunus besseyi* - Western Sand Cherry; Ann Lowdermilk, p. 15

PLANT NAME: *Prunus virginiana* - Chokecherry; Angela Overy, p. 11

PLANT NAME: *Quercus bicolor* - Swamp White Oak; Allyn Jarrett, p. 13

PLANT NAME: *Quercus macrocarpa* - Burr Oak; Allyn Jarrett, p. 8

PLANT NAME: *Rhus trilobata* - Three Leaf Sumac; Sandie Howard, p. 13

PLANT NAME: *Rhus typhina* - Staghorn Sumac; Sandie Howard, p. 14

PLANT NAME: *Robinia neomexicana* - New Mexico Locust; Marjorie C. Leggitt, p. 7

PLANT NAME: *Sophora japonica* - Japanese Pagoda Tree; Karen Boggs, p. 11

PLANT NAME: *Spirea* x *vanhouttei* - Vanhoutte Spirea; Linda Lorraine Wolfe, p. 14

PLANT NAME: *Syringa vulgaris* - Lilac; Linda Evans, p. 12

PLANT NAME: *Viburnum lantana* - Wayfaring Tree; Nancy Nelson, p. 16

PLANT NAME: *Yucca* species - Yucca; Susan Rubin, p. 8

PLANT NAME: *Rosa* x *harisonii* - Harison's Yellow Rose; Marie Orlin, p. 8

PLANT NAME: *Achillea* species - Yarrow; Tana Pittman, p. 19

PLANT NAME: *Agastache cana* - Dubble Bubble Mint; Jill Buck, p. 25

PLANT NAME: *Alyssoides utriculata* - Bladderpod; Jill Buck, p. 20

PLANT NAME: *Anacyclus depressus* - Atlas Daisy; Shirley Nelson, p. 18

PLANT NAME: *Asclepias tuberosa* - Butterfly Weed; Lori Rhea Swingle, p. 24

PLANT NAME: *Aurinia saxatile* - Basket-of-Gold; Allyn Jarrett, p. 20

PLANT NAME: *Callirhoe involucrata* - Wine Cup; Tanya McMurtry, p. 30

PLANT NAME: *Campanula rotundifolia* - Bluebell; Nancy Nelson, p. 27

PLANT NAME: *Centranthus ruber* - Red Valerian; Allyn Jarrett, p. 25

PLANT NAME: *Campsis radicans* - Trumpet Vine; Susan Rubin, p. 24

PLANT NAME: *Eriogonum umbellatum* - Sulphur Flower; Debbie Brown Tejada, p. 20

PLANT NAME: *Gaillardia aristata* - Blanketflower; Marie Orlin, p. 21

PLANT NAME: *Gutierrezia sarothrae* - Snakewweed; Susan Rubin, p. 21

PLANT NAME: *Hemerocallis* species - Daylily; Linda Lorraine Wolfe, p. 18

PLANT NAME: *Iris* hybrids - Bearded Iris; Ann Lowdermilk, p. 18

PLANT NAME: *Liatris punctata* - Gayfeather; Marie Orlin, p. 29

PLANT NAME: *Linum perenne* - Blue Flax; Marjorie C. Leggitt, p. 30

PLANT NAME: *Nepeta* x *faassenii* - Catmint; Cynthia Cano, p. 28

PLANT NAME: *Oenothera missouriensis* - Ozark Sundrop; Karen Boggs, p. 22

PLANT NAME: *Parthenocissus quinquefolia* - Virginia Creeper; Linda Evans, p. 31

PLANT NAME: *Perovskia atriplicifolia* - Russian Sage; Tanya Pittman, p. 31

PLANT NAME: *Penstemon* species - Penstemon; Angela Overy, p. 19

PLANT NAME: *Polygonum aubertii* - Silver Lace Vine; Cynthia Cano, p. 19

PLANT NAME: *Pulsatilla vulgaris* - European Pasqueflower; Linda Evans, p. 29

PLANT NAME: *Ratibida columnifera* - Prairie Coneflower; Angela Overy, p. 22

PLANT NAME: *Salvia officinalis* - Garden Sage; Debbie Brown Tejada, p. 30

PLANT NAME: *Stanleya pinnata* - Prince's Plume; Jill Buck, p. 23

PLANT NAME: *Tanacetum densum* - Partridge Feather; Susan Rubin, p. 23

PLANT NAME: *Zauschneria arizonica* - Arizona Zauschneria; Sandie Howard, p. 26

PLANT NAME: *Antennaria rosea* - Pink Pussytoes; Susan Rubin, p. 34

PLANT NAME: *Bouteloua curtipendula* - Sideoats Grama; Debbie Brown Tejada, p. 34

PLANT NAME: *Calamagrostis acutiflora* - Karl Foerster FRG; Nancy Nelson, p. 35

PLANT NAME: *Cerastium tomentosum* - Snow-in-Summer; Tanya McMurtry, p. 36

PLANT NAME: *Delosperma cooperi* - Pink Hardy Ice Plant; Angela Overy, p. 36

PLANT NAME: *Delosperma nubigenum* - Hardy Yellow Ice Plant; Angela Overy, p. 36

PLANT NAME: *Festuca ovina glauca* - Blue Fescue; Sandie Howard, p. 37

PLANT NAME: *Miscanthus sinensis* - Miscanthus Grass; Pamela Hoffman, p. 38

PLANT NAME: *Oryzopsis hymenoides* - Indian Rice Grass; Susan T. Fisher, p. 38

PLANT NAME: *Pennisetum alopecuroides* - Fountain Grass; Debbie Brown Tejada, p. 38

PLANT NAME: *Pennisetum setaceum* 'Rubrum' - Purple Fountain Grass; Debbie Brown Tejada, p. 39

PLANT NAME: *Santolina chamaecyparissus* - Lavender Cotton; Melody Durrett, p. 39

PLANT NAME: *Polygonum affine* - Himalayan Fleeceflower; Sandie Howard, p. 39

PLANT NAME: *Sedum spectabile* - Showy Stonecrop; Lynn Janicki, p. 40

PLANT NAME: *Sempervivum* species - Hens and Chicks; Susan Rubin, p. 40

PLANT NAME: *Thymus pseudolanuginosus* - Woolly Thyme; Marilyn Taylor, p. 40

PLANT NAME: *Veronica pectinata* - Blue Woolly Speedwell; Susan Rubin, p. 41

PLANT NAME: *Zinnia grandiflora* - Desert Zinnia; Marilyn Taylor, p. 41

PLANT NAME: *Coreopsis tinctoria* - Tickseed; Ann Lowdermilk, p. 44

PLANT NAME: *Cosmos sulphureus* - Yellow Cosmos; Karen Boggs, p. 45

PLANT NAME: *Cosmos bipinnatus* - Cosmos; Karen Boggs, p. 48

PLANT NAME: *Eschscholzia californica* - California Poppy; Tanya McMurtry, p. 47

PLANT NAME: *Gomphrena globosa* - Globe Amaranth; Tana Pittman, p. 44

PLANT NAME: *Lavatera trimestris* - Annual Mallow; Linda Evans, p. 51

PLANT NAME: *Portulaca grandiflora* - Moss Rose; Karen Boggs, p. 44

PLANT NAME: *Salvia sclarea* - Clary Sage; Debbie Brown Tejada, p. 53

PLANT NAME: *Sanvitalia procumbens* - Creeping Zinnia; Ann Lowdermilk, p. 46

PLANT NAME: *Tropaeolum majus* - Nasturtium; Lori Rhea Swingle, p. 46

PLANT NAME: *Zinnia angustifolia* - Narrow Leaf Zinnia; Angela Overy, p. 46

PLANT NAME: *Alchemilla mollis* - Lady's Mantle; Susan Rubin, p. 59

PLANT NAME: *Arctostaphylos uva-ursi* - Kinnikinnick; Nancy Nelson, p. 56

PLANT NAME: *Bergenia cordifolia* - Heartleaf Bergenia; Harriet Olds, p. 59

PLANT NAME: *Brunnera macrophylla* - Perennial Forget-Me-Not; Nancy Nelson, p. 59

PLANT NAME: *Calamintha grandiflora* - Beautiful Mint; Jayme S. Irvin, p. 60

PLANT NAME: *Campanula portenshlagiana* - Dalmation Bellflower; Cynthia Cano, p. 60

PLANT NAME: *Galium odoratum* - Sweet Woodruff; Marilyn Taylor, p. 60

PLANT NAME: *Heuchera sanguinea* - Corallbells; Linda Lorraine Wolfe, p. 61

PLANT NAME: *Lamium maculatum* - Spotted Dead Nettle; Libby Kyer, p. 61

PLANT NAME: *Mahonia repens* - Creeping Grape Holly; Jill Buck, p. 61

PLANT NAME: *Rosa glauca* - Redleaf Rose; Linda Evans, p. 57

PLANT NAME: *Ptelea trifoliata* - Wafer Ash; Susan Rubin, p. 56

PLANT NAME: *Ribes aureum* - Golden Currant; Jayme S. Irvin, p. 57

PLANT NAME: *Rubus deliciosus* - Thimbleberry; Patty Homs, p. 57

PLANT NAME: *Sedum spurium* - Two-row Stonecrop; Lynn Janicki, p. 62

PLANT NAME: *Stachys lanata* - Lamb's Ear; Tanya McMurtry, p. 62

PLANT NAME: *Symphoricarpos* x *chenaultii* - Chenault Coralberry; Tanya McMurtry, p. 58

Table of Contents

INTRODUCTION, vi

KEY TO *XERISCAPE COLOR GUIDE*, ix

TREES AND SHRUBS, 1

PERENNIALS AND VINES, 17

GROUNDCOVERS AND GRASSES, 33

ANNUALS, 43

SHADE PLANTS, 55

Introduction

The *Xeriscape Color Guide* is more valuable to gardeners and landscape designers than a color wheel is to painters. While landscape painters may capture a single great moment in time, landscape gardeners must create great moments that extend through all four seasons and well into the future. For gardeners, the real hallmark is creating a harmony of colors that evolve and change over time, and the *Xeriscape Color Guide* is important as a landscape tool in this regard. In addition, the guide also signifies the important progress being made toward educating and involving people in the process of reducing their landscape's water resource needs.

From a metaphorical perspective, *Xeriscape Plant Guide*, published in 1996, shows landscape designers the type of paint (plants) to put on the canvas. Now, *Xeriscape Color Guide* takes designers up to the next level by helping them select and arrange the colors of paint in ways that stimulate our senses, excite our emotions, and add to the earthly beauty around us. And, because both books are coordinated with each other, the value of each is enhanced. The user-friendly format and graphic artwork of the *Xeriscape Color Guide* helps novice gardeners achieve a professional look to their landscapes. Accomplished gardeners and professional landscapers will find new and refreshing ways to expand their plant palettes and to simplify their design and construction processes.

For people planning a landscape, either new or a renovation of an existing one, the design process usually begins with some vision of the finished product. This vision may be as simple as adding a mass of Basket-of-Gold (*Aurinia saxatile*) for a splash of spring color or as complex as a complete makeover of a backyard. In all cases, the challenge is to be able to communicate that vision to others. Such communication is important during the selection and future purchase of plants and other materials, during construction, and for ongoing maintenance. It is always fun to boast about your garden to friends and associates when they extend compliments about the success of your vision.

The landscape design process is involved. Generally, most find it helpful to break the design into smaller, logical pieces—building blocks, if you will—wherein each block represents a piece of information needed for the plan. For example, let's say one major building block is plant materials. This block is made up of other smaller blocks—one of trees, one of shrubs, one of flowers, and so forth—each of which may typically include information, or sub-blocks, on the size, shape, color, and other attributes of the plant. Another major block is the exposure of the landscape to the sun throughout the year.

Once each block is fully identified, it may be reassembled with other blocks. Together these may act as a list of needs, a set of steps to follow, or even a drawing on paper. All of these are guides to help others share in the vision.

One of the key first steps, or blocks, necessary in the process of completing that vision is consideration of the function of the site. Just like a building is designed to fit the needs and personalities of its occupants, so too must the landscape. Buildings have rooms for specific purposes or functions. The rooms might include a kitchen, bathrooms and bedrooms, hallways and stairs for circulation, offices, conference rooms, or storage places. In the landscape there are needs for circulation routes and other rooms for specific outdoor uses. Creating areas for relaxation, entertaining, playing, growing food, privacy, socializing, or conducting business all add to the success of a landscape.

Once the "rooms" of the landscape have been decided upon and the arrangement of them made so there is flow and practicality in the design, the inanimate structures may be added. Such structures may include walks, steps, plazas or patios, retaining walls, water features, compost bins, garden sculptures, all of which add character and personality to the landscape.

At this point, the real fun begins and the landscape comes alive! When plants, especially larger trees and shrubs, are inserted into the design process, they usually become part of the landscape structure. Trees, like concrete, are relatively permanent parts of the landscape. Their location, mass, shape, and texture all help define areas of the landscape and tie these areas together. Trees and shrubs are often used as living walls of landscape rooms. Because of their greater permanence, it is crucial that these larger living parts of the landscape be selected for their spring, summer, fall, and winter colors as well as for their other attributes. A good first stop in the *Xeriscape Color Guide* will be trees and shrubs.

Older landscapes also benefit from a similar review process. Perhaps the landscape has a new owner with new needs or wants. Perhaps the original plants have overgrown their space or have declined in health. New species and cultivars of plants have been introduced over the years to the benefit of all landscapes. As an example, many residential landscapes of the early twentieth century were on small sites. Yet, the tree species available then were generally very massive at maturity and now, decades later, tend to overpower both the house and the site. For example, an old, massive, hard-to-maintain Silver Maple may be ready for replacement with a smaller Ginnala or Wasatch Maple.

Replacing massive aging and declining trees with more recently developed smaller species adds new dimension and image to these landscapes. And, because they are smaller at maturity, the cost to care for them and for their water consumption will be substantially less. A site that is dominated by an enclosure can be given a new feeling of openness, thus creating new vistas. The *Xeriscape Color Guide* and *Xeriscape Plant Guide* should be consulted at each decision point in the plant selection process.

The best part of landscape gardening is the selection of flowering annuals and perennials. Most perennials can be moved or changed easily from time to time to create evolving landscape images. Plants may be given or traded among friends and neighbors. New species and varieties are being developed and old favorites are being improved all the time. Many of these can be found in these two books.

The whimsy, the expression of personality, the accessorizing of the landscape, the ambiance and flair—all are associated with the selection and arrangement of flowers. Flowers have the dramatic final touch. They provide the contrast, the bold statement, the subtle texture, the hint of fragrance, the movement in the breeze, the calming hues vital to quality landscapes. The secret to successfully using plants together in the landscape is made easier by following the keys and charts in the color guide.

Visualize that newly completed project. The breakfast nook room extends out from the sliding glass door onto the new deck. Beyond the deck and through the warming sun of early morning the gray-striped bark of a multi-stemmed Amur Maple peeks out of the shadows. The scarlet Samoras soon yield with the onset of fall, their clusters of red blending with the red leaves of fall. It is twenty feet across the Blue Grama grass lawn from the deck to the focal point planting of the maple tree, shrubs, and perennials. The viewing angle from seats on the deck makes the yellow tops of Rabbitbrush at the edge of the deck appear to be part of the masses of Blue Mist Spirea flanking either side of the maple. Soon the soft green of the grass will change to the buff of winter, highlighted by the changing hues of the Mahonia at its edge. Clusters of Daylilies have long since lost their magnificent blooms, remaining as masses of gracefully arching grasslike blades of medium green. Red Valerian has bloomed for the second time and is beginning to fade. Spring will repeat the bold yellow color now on the Rabbitbrush across the lawn in the perennials as the Basket of Gold spring to life once again. Here is a garden with a simple yet effective use of a few species, a creative simplicity that is reflective in a quote from Henrich Heine:

> *Like a great poet, nature produces the greatest*
> *results with the simplest means. There are*
> *simply sun, flowers, water, and love.*

How does all of this fit into the overall concept of XERISCAPE™? Easily! Simplicity and beauty are two key premises that guided the original team of landscape architects, contractors, horticulturists, irrigation specialists, and Colorado State University Cooperative Extension representatives responsible for developing the XERISCAPE™ concept in 1981.

The first task undertaken by that group was the construction of a demonstration and education garden, a place to tantalize the human senses with the many colors, fragrances, and textures. This education garden permits people to experience firsthand "water conservation through creative landscaping." It presents many real possibilities and opportunities for people to make their own space on Mother Earth, however small, more compatible with nature. It is a garden that allows individuals the freedom to make positive decisions through their own experiences and always-growing level of knowledge about plants; a garden that helps them learn how to use less water and how to have a more sustainable future in their landscapes.

Since publication of the plant guide there are nearly two dozen Xeriscape™ gardens in Colorado alone. Additional gardens may be visited in nearly every state in the country and in countries as far away as Australia and Israel. A visit to any of these gardens is a rewarding experience.

While gardens provide real living examples during the visitation, the color guide provides a convenient and immediate reference to many of these same plants in the absence of such a garden.

The simplicity of the XERISCAPE™ concept exists in its seven fundamentals: The first fundamental is planning and design. The essence of this introduction has been about planning and design. An actual design would logically go into greater depth. The second fundamental is soil improvement. The third, turf alternatives describes how different types of turf and the reduction of an area of turf can help reduce water needs of the landscape. Using mulches is another fundamental, as is efficient irrigation. The sixth fundamental is appropriate maintenance. The last fundamental, the one that puts the "fun" in fundamental, is selecting and zoning of low-water requiring plants. One way plant selection has been simplified even further is by providing the *Xeriscape Color Guide*, and your adventure is about to begin.

Key to Xeriscape Color Guide

THE SEASONS

The page construction of this book is designed for fast reference. There are three plants depicted on each page. There are four horizontal sections per plant. These horizontal sections represent "spring," "summer," "autumn," and "winter." The format for these seasonal margins do not change throughout the book.

COLOR CHART

This is only a guide. The seasons of growth, flowering, fruiting, and dormancy are dependent upon the weather in any one year. The time for each phase may vary from this chart but should generally follow the sequence depicted.

 flowers—may cover the whole plant and will fill the whole space; if they are just part of the plant or if they become less significant as the season progresses they will fill a correspondingly smaller area.

 leaves—will be depicted as they change during the seasons and in proportion to the number of flowers or stems predominate during each of the four seasons.

 fruit—will follow the same pattern as the flowers and leaves.

 stems—are a significant part of trees, shrubs, and vines during the winter and are important in planning for color and texture. Perennials and annuals usually die back to the ground during the cold months, leaving that part of the landscape blank.

MAXIMUM ELEVATION

This is not an absolute value but a general guide. Plant hardiness at any elevation is dependent upon a balance of environmental factors, such as the high and low temperatures, wind, sun exposure, moisture, and so on. Plants can be found higher than the listed elevation depending upon these factors. Specific elevations given in this book are meant as a guideline.

WATER

The first water drop icon is the preferred amount of water required by the plant. The second water drop icon, if necessary, is the amount of water the plant will adapt to over time.

 low—means watering is required infrequently and only during extended dry periods in the summer.

 moderate—means watering is required regularly but not frequently.

 higher—means water must be applied regularly and frequently.

EXPOSURE

The first sun icon is the preferred exposure. The second, if necessary, represents exposures in the order of most tolerable.

 **full sun**—all day

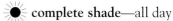 **part-day shade**—or filtered shade

 **complete shade**—all day

FORM

Form definitions give the reader a general look at how the plant will mature and change through the seasons.

LANDSCAPE USE

This section is provided to give suggestions on how plants may be used in a garden design, such as a hedge or border. The purpose of this information is to better facilitate the plant useage in an overall landscape.

PAGE REFERENCE

Xeriscape Color Guide is meant to be a handy addendum to the *Xeriscape Plant Guide*. Page numbers refer to more in-depth descriptions found in the *Xeriscape Plant Guide*.

Spring

Summer

Autumn

Winter

Spring

Summer

Autumn

Winter

Spring

Summer

Autumn

Winter

Trees and Shrubs

Amorpha canescens—Leadplant

Fabaceae—Pea Family
Deciduous Shrub
Height: 1 to 4 feet • Spread: 3 to 4 feet

MAXIMUM ELEVATION: 5,500 feet.

WATER: **EXPOSURE:**

FORM: Erect, slightly arching stems with an open, spreading habit, fernlike.

LANDSCAPE USE: A good hardy shrub for sunny locations and well-drained soils.

PAGE REFERENCE: 10 and 11.

Atriplex canescens—Fourwing Saltbush, Chamiso

Chenopodiaceae—Goosefoot Family
Semievergreen Shrub
Height: 1 to 6 feet • Spread: 4 to 8 feet

MAXIMUM ELEVATION: Grasslands, shrub lands, and plateaus at 4,500- to 7,000-foot elevations in Colorado. Occurs in New Mexico, north to South Dakota, west to California from sea level to 8,000 feet.

WATER: **EXPOSURE:**

FORM: Stout stems, densely branched, forming a rounded mound.

LANDSCAPE USE: Tall ground cover, low hedge or screen, dry parkway or road median, barrier. Good background for intense flower colors.

PAGE REFERENCE: 12 and 13.

Caryopteris x clandonensis—Blue Mist Spirea

Verbenaceae—Verbena Family
Deciduous Shrub
Height: 2 to 3 feet • Spread: 3 feet

MAXIMUM ELEVATION: good to 8,500 feet in Colorado.

WATER: **EXPOSURE:**

FORM: Loosely rounded, erect with a soft appearance.

LANDSCAPE USE: May be used as a shrub or perennial in mixed borders. Best appearance when several are massed together or used with other plants.

PAGE REFERENCE: 14 and 15.

Ceratoides lanata—Winterfat, White Sage

Chenopodiaceae—Goosefoot Family
Perennial Subshrub
Height: 1 to 3 feet • Spread: 2 to 4 feet

MAXIMUM ELEVATION: 10,000 feet in the mountains of central Utah.

WATER: ○ ◐ **EXPOSURE:** ☼

FORM: Open, upright or bending, herbaceous stems arising from a woody base.

LANDSCAPE USE: Foreground to deep green foliage plants, naturalized areas mixed with grasses or as a background to colorful ground covers.

PAGE REFERENCE: 20 and 21.

Cercocarpus ledifolius— Curl-leaf Mountain-Mahogany

Roseaceae—Rose Family • Broadleaf Evergreen Shrub or Small Tree
Height: 4 to 15 feet • Spread: 4 to 8 feet

MAXIMUM ELEVATION: 9,000 feet in AZ, CA, UT, and ID.

WATER: ○ **EXPOSURE:** ☼ ◐

FORM: Erect, irregular, loosely vase-shaped and densely branched to the ground. Also grown as a single-stem tree or multi-stem clump tree. Can be pruned into a hedge.

LANDSCAPE USE: Attractive as a focal interest. Good evergreen for small yards or spaces. Appropriate as low-water foundation plant.

PAGE REFERENCE: 22 and 23.

Chamaebatiaria millefolium—Fernbush

Rosaceae—Rose Family
Semi-evergreen Shrub
Height: 4 to 6 feet • Spread: 4 to 6 feet

MAXIMUM ELEVATION: up to 7,000 feet in Colorado.

WATER: ○ **EXPOSURE:** ☼

FORM: Upright, fuzzy stems splay out from the center forming a rounded or somewhat irregular habit.

LANDSCAPE USE: Midsummer accent, unshorn hedge, screen, planted in mass.

PAGE REFERENCE: 24 and 25.

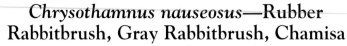

Chrysothamnus nauseosus—Rubber Rabbitbrush, Gray Rabbitbrush, Chamisa

Asteraceae—Sunflower Family
Deciduous Shrub
Height: 2 to 6 feet • Spread: 2 to 4 feet

MAXIMUM ELEVATION: 9,000 feet in Colorado.

WATER: **EXPOSURE:**

FORM: Irregular globe-shaped, multi-stemmed, woody base with herbaceous stems. Plant has a soft natural appearance in the landscape.

LANDSCAPE USE: Very dry areas; good for traffic islands, south-facing slopes.

PAGE REFERENCE: 26 and 27.

Cowania mexicana—Cliffrose, Quinine Bush

Rosaceae—Rose Family
Broadleaf Evergreen Shrub
Height: 3 to 12 feet • Spread: 3 to 6 feet

MAXIMUM ELEVATION: up to 7,000 feet in Colorado.

WATER: 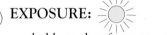 **EXPOSURE:**

FORM: Rigid, gnarled branches form an upright, rather open shrub.

LANDSCAPE USE: Background for perennials or among perennials because it casts light shade. Excellent as an untrimmed hedge or as a specimen in a dry garden. Ideal for naturalized landscapes. Can be sheared into a hedge.

PAGE REFERENCE: 30 and 31.

Cytisus scoparius 'Moonlight'— Moonlight Broom, Scotch Broom

Fabaceae—Pea Family
Deciduous Shrub
Height: 4 to 6 feet • Spread: 4 to 6 feet

MAXIMUM ELEVATION: good to 7,000 feet in Colorado.

WATER: **EXPOSURE:**

FORM: Erect, upright mass of wandlike, bright green stems.

LANDSCAPE USE: Use as a vertical contrast to softer, bushier plants. Plant as a screen or hedge along fences, driveways, and paths. Mix with perennials in a border.

PAGE REFERENCE: 47.

Fallugia paradoxa—Apache Plume

Rosaceae—Rose Family
Deciduous Shrub
Height: 3 to 5 feet • Spread: 3 to 5 feet

MAXIMUM ELEVATION: up to 8,000 feet from Utah south to Texas.

WATER: 💧 **EXPOSURE:** ☀

FORM: Lacy appearing mound with dense, slender branches.

LANDSCAPE USE: Fine-textured shrub valuable for dry spots in the garden. Also useful for erosion control and wildlife forage. Provides cover for small mammals and ground-dwelling birds. Best used in massings along highways.

PAGE REFERENCE: 34 and 35.

Hippophae rhamnoides—Sea Buckthorn

Elaeagnaceae—Oleaster Family
Deciduous Shrub
Height: 8 to 18 feet • Spread: 8 to 12 feet

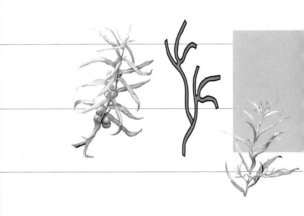

MAXIMUM ELEVATION: up to 7,000 feet in Colorado.

WATER: 💧 **EXPOSURE:** ☀

FORM: Erect, thorny shrub.

LANDSCAPE USE: Informal background, barrier plant or hedge, wildlife, naturalizing.

PAGE REFERENCE: 42 and 43.

Juniperus horizontalis—Creeping Juniper

Cupressaceae—Cypress Family
Evergreen Shrub
Height: 6 to 18 inches • Spread: 5 to 8 feet

MAXIMUM ELEVATION: up to 8,000 feet in Colorado.

WATER: 💧💧 **EXPOSURE:** ☀

FORM: Low spreader, usually prostrate, sometimes upright.

LANDSCAPE USE: Ground cover, coverage or hillside or bank, cascade over rock wall or in planters.

PAGE REFERENCE: 44 and 45.

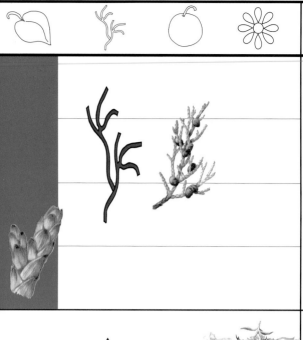

Juniperus scopulorum—Rocky Mountain Juniper
Cupressaceae—Cypress Family
Evergreen Tree or Large Shrub
Height: up to 30 feet in Colorado • Spread: 8 to 15 feet

MAXIMUM ELEVATION: up to 10,000 feet in Colorado.

WATER: **EXPOSURE:**

FORM: Widely variable growth habit but generally pyramidal, often with several main stems.

LANDSCAPE USE: Use as screens, hedges, background specimens. Birds use as shelter and eat the fruit.

PAGE REFERENCE: 46.

Kolkwitzia amabilis—Beauty Bush
Caprifoliaceae—Honeysuckle Family
Deciduous Shrub
Height: 6 to 10 feet • Spread: 4 to 8 feet

MAXIMUM ELEVATION: good to 7,000 feet in Colorado.

WATER: **EXPOSURE:**

FORM: Finely branched, multiple upright stems grow outward to form a dense shrub with a broad, rounded habit.

LANDSCAPE USE: Best in a shrub border rather than used as a specimen plant. Plant near enough to a walk that the early summer flower show can be appreciated.

PAGE REFERENCE: 48 and 49.

Pinus aristata—Bristlecone Pine, Foxtail Pine
Pinaceae—Pine Family
Alpine Conifer
Height: 20 to 30 feet • Spread: 10 to 15 feet

MAXIMUM ELEVATION: up to 10,800 feet in Colorado, Utah, Nevada and California.

WATER: **EXPOSURE:**

FORM: Trunk is short, stocky and contorted; dense crown; irregular spreading branches; shrubby in appearance. More open as tree matures.

LANDSCAPE USE: Specimen, evergreen hedge, parks, naturalization.

PAGE REFERENCE: 52.

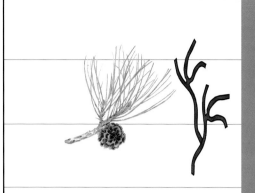

Pinus ponderosa—Ponderosa Pine, Western Yellow Pine

Pinaceae—Pine Family
Conifer Tree
Height: 80 to 100 feet • Spread: 25 to 30 feet

MAXIMUM ELEVATION: up to 9,000 feet in Colorado.

WATER: ⬠   **EXPOSURE:** ☼

FORM: Narrow, pyramidal, tightly packed with branches when young.

LANDSCAPE USE: Native planting; mass or group plantings; windbreak or a focal point in the landscape.

PAGE REFERENCE: 53.

Potentilla fruticosa—Bush Cinquefoil, Potentilla, Shrubby Cinquefoil

Rosaceae—Rose Family
Deciduous Shrub
Height: 1 to 4 feet • Spread: 2 to 4 feet

MAXIMUM ELEVATION: 10,000 feet.

WATER: ⬠⬠   **EXPOSURE:** ☼ ◐

FORM: Upright or arching stems densely covered with foliage, forming a low, rounded bush.

LANDSCAPE USE: Shrub border; mass planting; informal hedges; mixed perennial border.

PAGE REFERENCE: 54 and 55.

Robinia neomexicana—New Mexico Locust, Rose Locust

Fabaceae—Pea Family
Deciduous Shrub or Small Tree
Height: 6 to 20 feet • Spread: 10 to 20 feet

MAXIMUM ELEVATION: 8,500 feet.

WATER: ⬠⬠   **EXPOSURE:** ☼

FORM: Thicket-forming large shrub or small tree with irregular, rigid branches armed with paired thorns.

LANDSCAPE USE: Beautiful flower; useful as windbreak or hedge. Favorable for stabilizing soil on hillsides.

PAGE REFERENCE: 70 and 71.

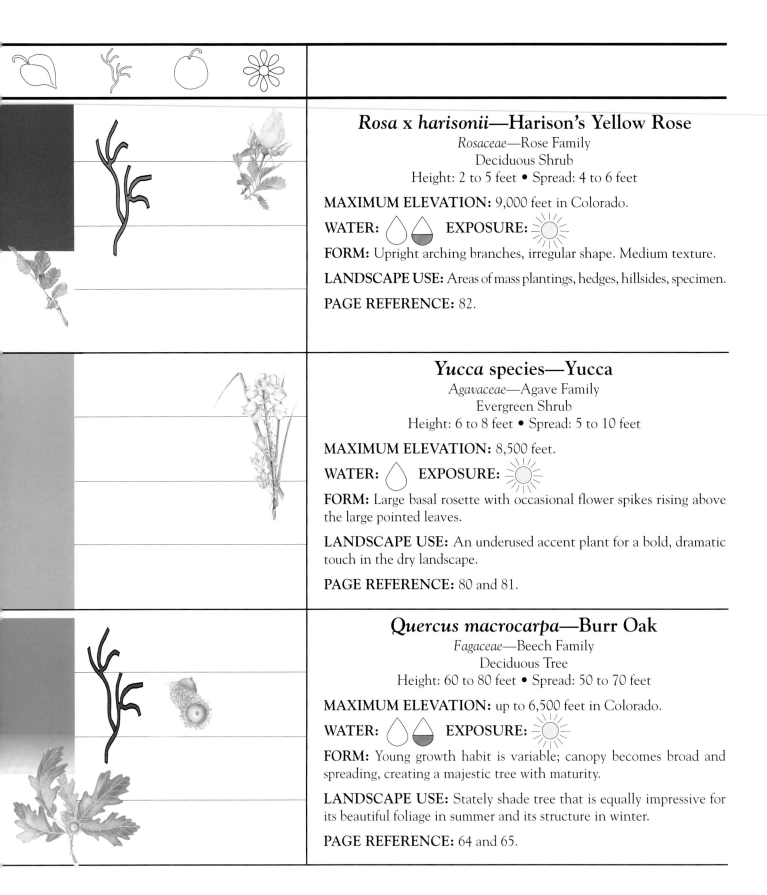

Rosa x harisonii—Harison's Yellow Rose

Rosaceae—Rose Family
Deciduous Shrub
Height: 2 to 5 feet • Spread: 4 to 6 feet

MAXIMUM ELEVATION: 9,000 feet in Colorado.

WATER: **EXPOSURE:**

FORM: Upright arching branches, irregular shape. Medium texture.

LANDSCAPE USE: Areas of mass plantings, hedges, hillsides, specimen.

PAGE REFERENCE: 82.

Yucca species—Yucca

Agavaceae—Agave Family
Evergreen Shrub
Height: 6 to 8 feet • Spread: 5 to 10 feet

MAXIMUM ELEVATION: 8,500 feet.

WATER: **EXPOSURE:**

FORM: Large basal rosette with occasional flower spikes rising above the large pointed leaves.

LANDSCAPE USE: An underused accent plant for a bold, dramatic touch in the dry landscape.

PAGE REFERENCE: 80 and 81.

Quercus macrocarpa—Burr Oak

Fagaceae—Beech Family
Deciduous Tree
Height: 60 to 80 feet • Spread: 50 to 70 feet

MAXIMUM ELEVATION: up to 6,500 feet in Colorado.

WATER: **EXPOSURE:**

FORM: Young growth habit is variable; canopy becomes broad and spreading, creating a majestic tree with maturity.

LANDSCAPE USE: Stately shade tree that is equally impressive for its beautiful foliage in summer and its structure in winter.

PAGE REFERENCE: 64 and 65.

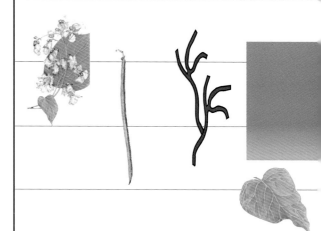

Catalpa speciosa—
Western Catalpa, Northern Catalpa

Bignoniaceaea—Trumpet Creeper Family
Deciduous Tree
Height: 40 to 70 feet • Spread: 20 to 40 feet

MAXIMUM ELEVATION: good to 6,000 feet in Colorado.

WATER: **EXPOSURE:**

FORM: Large, upright branches form an irregular, open crown. Coarse textured, summer and winter.

LANDSCAPE USE: Specimen, shade; parks, street.

PAGE REFERENCE: 16 and 17.

Celtis occidentalis—Common Hackberry

Ulmaceae—Elm Family
Deciduous Tree
Height: 50 to 60 feet • Spread: 40 to 50 feet

MAXIMUM ELEVATION: good to 7,000 feet in Colorado.

WATER: **EXPOSURE:**

FORM: Upright branches arch to create a high, dense canopy in a broad oval shape.

LANDSCAPE USE: Street tree, shade, parking islands, windbreak. Easy to establish on sites where it may be difficult for other trees to grow.

PAGE REFERENCE: 18 and 19.

Forestiera neomexicana—New Mexican Privet, Adelia, Desert Olive

Oleaceae—Olive Family
Deciduous Shrub
Height: 12 to 15 feet • Spread: 6 to 10 feet

MAXIMUM ELEVATION: 7,000 feet.

WATER: **EXPOSURE:**

FORM: Upright, multi-stemmed, finely twigged branches create a dense, rounded shrub.

LANDSCAPE USE: Attractive informal hedge; excellent sheared hedge; provides good screen when fast results are needed. Wildlife habitat.

PAGE REFERENCE: 36 and 37.

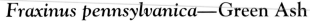

Fraxinus pennsylvanica—Green Ash

Oleaceae—Olive Family
Deciduous Tree
Height: 50 to 60 feet • Spread: 30 to 40 feet

MAXIMUM ELEVATION: 7,500 feet in Colorado.

WATER: **EXPOSURE:**

FORM: When young, rather open and pyramidal; mature are irregular oval or rounded and spreading. Coarse texture in the landscape, especially in winter.

LANDSCAPE USE: Street border, specimen, grove or tall screen, summer shade, and windbreak.

PAGE REFERENCE: 38 and 39.

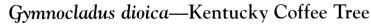

Gymnocladus dioica—Kentucky Coffee Tree

Fabaceae—Pea Family
Deciduous Tree
Height: 50 to 60 feet • Spread: 30 to 40 feet

MAXIMUM ELEVATION: up to 8,000 feet in Colorado.

WATER: **EXPOSURE:**

FORM: Erect, rounded crown. Young trees are narrow and irregularly shaped. Trees broaden with age, having several large, ascending branches and fewer lateral branches.

LANDSCAPE USE: Specimen tree or street tree.

PAGE REFERENCE: 40 and 41.

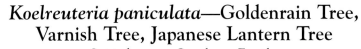

Koelreuteria paniculata—Goldenrain Tree, Varnish Tree, Japanese Lantern Tree

Sapindaceae—Soapberry Family
Deciduous Tree
Height: 20 to 30 feet • Spread: 25 to 30 feet

MAXIMUM ELEVATION: 6,000 feet.

WATER: **EXPOSURE:**

FORM: Spreading, ascending branches with an open, rounded crown.

LANDSCAPE USE: Accent, specimen or focal interest for small landscapes. Good smaller tree for under power lines.

PAGE REFERENCE: 50 and 51.

Prunus armeniaca—Apricot

Rosaceae—Rose Family
Deciduous Tree
Height: 15 to 30 feet • Spread: 20 to 30 feet

MAXIMUM ELEVATION: up to 7,000 feet in Colorado.

WATER: **EXPOSURE:**

FORM: Handsome, wide spreading, rounded, open crown.

LANDSCAPE USE: Small tree for small landscapes; excellent dappled shade source; outstanding early spring ornamental accent.

PAGE REFERENCE: 56 and 57.

Prunus virginiana—Chokecherry

Rosaceae—Rose Family
Large Shrub or Small Tree
Height: 20 to 30 feet • Spread: 10 to 25 feet

MAXIMUM ELEVATION: 10,000 feet.

WATER: 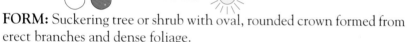 **EXPOSURE:**

FORM: Suckering tree or shrub with oval, rounded crown formed from erect branches and dense foliage.

LANDSCAPE USE: Useful as specimen when kept pruned or as a clump tree or large shrub. Also appropriate for hedging, screening, naturalizing, and attracting wildlife.

PAGE REFERENCE: 60 and 61.

Sophora japonica—Japanese Pagoda Tree, Chinese or Japanese Scholar Tree

Fabaceae—Pea Family
Deciduous Tree
Height: 40 to 60 feet • Spread: 40 to 60 feet

MAXIMUM ELEVATION: 6,000 feet.

WATER: **EXPOSURE:**

FORM: Upward spreading branches that form an oval to rounded crown. Casts light shade.

LANDSCAPE USE: Medium-sized tree, good for city conditions and poor soil. One of the few trees flowering in late summer.

PAGE REFERENCE: 72 and 73.

Syringa vulgaris—Common Lilac

Oleaceae—Olive Family
Deciduous Shrub
Height: 8 to 20 feet at maturity • Spread: 6 to 15 feet at maturity

MAXIMUM ELEVATION: 11,000 feet.

WATER: **EXPOSURE:**

FORM: Strong multi-stemmed branches form an upright, vase-shaped or rounded shrub.

LANDSCAPE USE: Shrub borders, groupings, shelterbelts, specimens.

PAGE REFERENCE: 76 and 77.

Aesculus glabra—Ohio Buckeye, Fetid Buckeye

Hippocastanaceae—Horsechestnut Family
Deciduous Tree
Height: 25 to 35 feet • Spread: 12 to 25 feet

MAXIMUM ELEVATION: 6,000 feet.

WATER: **EXPOSURE:**

FORM: Strong, ascending branches form a dense, rounded to broad oval tree. Coarse textured in the landscape.

LANDSCAPE USE: Shade, specimen, screen, windbreak; excellent for a small yard.

PAGE REFERENCE: 6 and 7.

Crataegus crus-galli—Cockspur Hawthorn

Rosaceae—Rose Family
Deciduous Small Tree or Large Shrub
Height: 20 to 30 feet • Spread: 20 to 35 feet

MAXIMUM ELEVATION: 8,000 feet.

WATER: **EXPOSURE:**

FORM: Round top with unique horizontal branching often growing low to the ground. Distinct habit makes it easy to identify.

LANDSCAPE USE: Specimen plant, informal grouping or as screens, hedges or barriers.

PAGE REFERENCE: 32 and 33.

Acer ginnala—Amur Maple, Ginnala Maple
Aceraceae—Maple Family
Small Tree or Shrub
Height: 15 to 20 feet • Spread: 15 to 20 feet, single- or multi-trunked

MAXIMUM ELEVATION: 8,500 feet.

WATER: ◌ ◌ **EXPOSURE:** ☀ ◑

FORM: Round to irregular shape. Small tree may be single- or multi-stemmed.

LANDSCAPE USE: Excellent specimen tree for small yards or patios, or for grouping, massing, or screening. Good small tree under power lines.

PAGE REFERENCE: 2 and 3.

Quercus bicolor—Swamp White Oak
Fagaceae—Beech Family
Deciduous Tree
Height: 40 to 50 feet • Spread: 30 to 50 feet

MAXIMUM ELEVATION: 6,000 feet in Colorado.

WATER: ◉ ◌ **EXPOSURE:** ☀ ◑

FORM: Lower branches on a short-trunked tree are descending while upper branches are more erect, creating a broad, somewhat open, conical to rounded crown. Medium texture in the landscape.

LANDSCAPE USE: Shade tree.

PAGE REFERENCE: 62 and 63.

Rhus trilobata—Three Leaf Sumac, Skunkbush, Lemonade Sumac, Squawbush
Anacardiaceae—Cashew Family
Deciduous Shrub
Height: 3 to 6 feet • Spread: 3 to 6 feet

MAXIMUM ELEVATION: 9,000 feet.

WATER: ◌ ◌ **EXPOSURE:** ☀ ◑

FORM: Rigid, arching branches form dense, round shrub.

LANDSCAPE USE: Dry shrub borders, barrier plantings, or naturalistic settings. Appropriate for erosion control on difficult sites such as roadsides and steep banks.

PAGE REFERENCE: 66 and 67.

Rhus typhina—Staghorn Sumac

Anacardiaceae—Cashew Family
Deciduous Shrub
Height: 8 to 10 feet • Spread: 8 to 15 feet

MAXIMUM ELEVATION: 7,500 feet.

WATER: ◯   **EXPOSURE:** ☀

FORM: Open, loose, spreading shrub with a flattish crown.

LANDSCAPE USE: Good for massing, banks, waste areas, naturalizing. Large planter boxes where it can sucker freely. Not recommended as a specimen or foundation plant.

PAGE REFERENCE: 68 and 69.

Spiraea x vanhouttei—Vanhoutte Spirea

Rosaceae—Rose Family
Deciduous Shrub
Height: 6 to 8 feet • Spread: 5 to 10 feet

MAXIMUM ELEVATION: 7,500 feet.

WATER: ◯ ◗   **EXPOSURE:** ☀ ◑

FORM: Fine-textured, medium-sized shrub with an elegant fountainlike shape.

LANDSCAPE USE: Specimen plant, informal hedge, or mass planting.

PAGE REFERENCE: 74 and 75.

Acer grandidentatum— Bigtooth Maple, Wasatch Maple, Rocky Mountain Sugar Maple

Aceraceae—Maple Family
Deciduous Tree
Height: 20 to 30 feet • Spread: 20 to 30 feet

MAXIMUM ELEVATION: 8,000 feet.

WATER: ◯ ◗   **EXPOSURE:** ☀ ◑

FORM: Usually multi-stemmed, broad, rounded with upright rigid branches.

LANDSCAPE USE: Small specimen tree, large shrub for screening.

PAGE REFERENCE: 4 and 5.

Amelanchier alnifolia— Saskatoon Serviceberry, Rocky Mountain Serviceberry, Western Serviceberry

Hippocastanaceae—Rose Family
Multi-stemmed Shrub or Small Tree
Height: 10 to 12 feet • Spread: 20 feet

MAXIMUM ELEVATION: 10,000 feet.

WATER: ○ **EXPOSURE:** ☼ ◑

FORM: Upright, arching branches forming a rounded crown.

LANDSCAPE USE: Use as a specimen plant, hedge, in shrub or mixed border; fits nicely in a naturalistic setting. Attractive to wildlife.

PAGE REFERENCE: 8 and 9.

Cotoneaster divaricatus—Spreading Cotoneaster

Rosaceae—Rose Family
Deciduous Shrub
Height: 3 to 5 feet • Spread: 6 to 8 feet

MAXIMUM ELEVATION: 8,500 feet.

WATER: ○ ◐ **EXPOSURE:** ☼ ◑

FORM: Wide spreading with upright, arching stems originating from the center. Stems are trimmed with small leaves.

LANDSCAPE USE: Use as boundary, informal hedge or screen, large bank planting, foundation planting. They are especially attractive spilling over a wall or rocks.

PAGE REFERENCE: 28 and 29.

Prunus besseyi—Western Sand Cherry, Hanson's Bush Cherry

Rosaceae—Rose Family
Deciduous Shrub
Height: 4 to 6 feet • Spread: 4 to 6 feet

MAXIMUM ELEVATION: up to 8,000 feet in Colorado.

WATER: ○ ◐ **EXPOSURE:** ☼

FORM: Spreading, open, airy, upright branches forming a rounded or vaselike shape.

LANDSCAPE USE: Foundation plant, wildlife, massing, background border plant.

PAGE REFERENCE: 58 and 59.

Viburnum lantana—Wayfaring Tree, Viburnum

Caprifoliaceae—Honeysuckle Family
Deciduous Shrub
Height: 10 to 15 feet • Spread: 10 to 15 feet

MAXIMUM ELEVATION: 8,000 feet.

WATER: **EXPOSURE:**

FORM: Thick spreading branches forming a rounded profile, coarse winter appearance.

LANDSCAPE USE: Informal hedge, screen or in a mixed shrub or perennial border, specimen plant, or shelterbelt.

PAGE REFERENCE: 78 and 79.

PLANTING PLAN—SITTING STONE OASIS

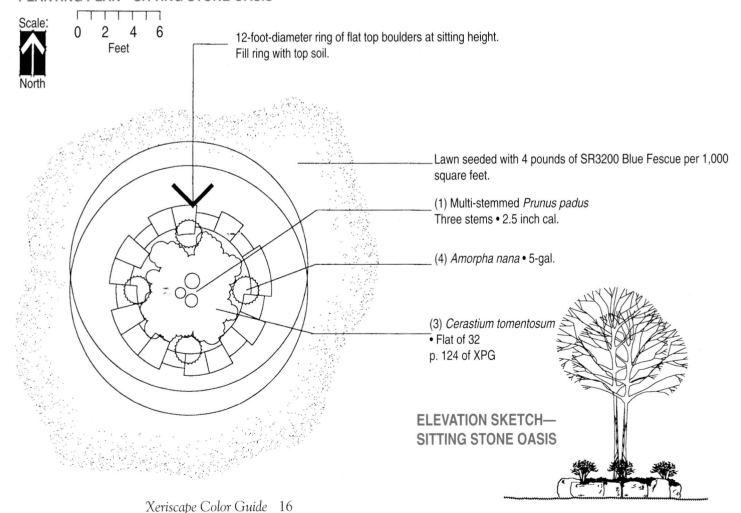

Scale:

0   2   4   6
Feet

North

12-foot-diameter ring of flat top boulders at sitting height. Fill ring with top soil.

Lawn seeded with 4 pounds of SR3200 Blue Fescue per 1,000 square feet.

(1) Multi-stemmed *Prunus padus*
Three stems • 2.5 inch cal.

(4) *Amorpha nana* • 5-gal.

(3) *Cerastium tomentosum*
• Flat of 32
p. 124 of XPG

**ELEVATION SKETCH—
SITTING STONE OASIS**

Perennials
and Vines

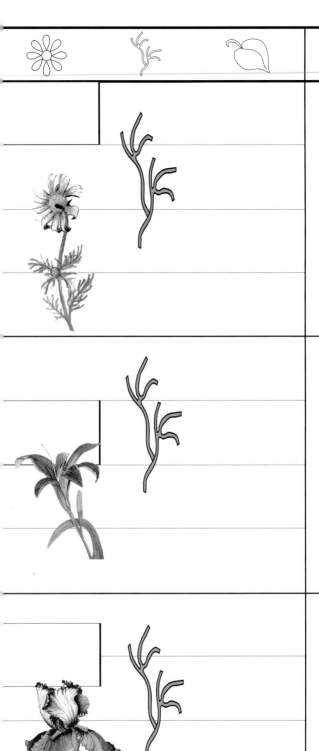

Anacyclus depressus—Atlas Daisy
Asteraceae—Sunflower Family
Herbaceous Perennial
Height: 3 inches • Spread: 15 inches

MAXIMUM ELEVATION: 10,000 feet.

WATER: **EXPOSURE:**

FORM: Prostate, dense.

LANDSCAPE USE: Good in dry rock gardens, front of dry borders, ground cover; especially attractive hanging over the edge of a wall.

PAGE REFERENCE: 88.

Hemerocallis species—Daylily
Liliaceae—Lily Family
Herbaceous Perennial
Height: 1 to 6 feet, (usually about 3½ feet) • Spread: 1 to 3 feet

MAXIMUM ELEVATION: 10,000 feet.

WATER: **EXPOSURE:**

FORM: Large clumps of arching bladelike leaves with flower stems rising above the clump.

LANDSCAPE USE: Versatile. Plant in mass, in mixed borders, on slopes as a tall ground cover, as an informal hedge, or in a cluster as specimen plants.

PAGE REFERENCE: 99.

Iris hybrids—Bearded Iris, German Iris, Flag, The Rainbow Flower, Poor Man's Orchid
Iridaceae—Iris Family • Perennial
Height: leaves—1½ feet tall, flower stems—2 to 3 feet
Spread: 1½ to 2 feet+

MAXIMUM ELEVATION: 8,500 feet.

WATER: **EXPOSURE:**

FORM: Clumps of erect swordlike leaves arranged in a fanlike pattern with stems and flowers rising above.

LANDSCAPE USE: An accent along the border or fences and walls, in rock gardens and for early color after spring bulbs have finished.

PAGE REFERENCE: 100 and 101.

Penstemon species—Penstemon, Beardtongue

Scroplulariaceae—Snapdragon Family
Herbaceous Perennial
Height: 4 to 48 inches • Spread: 3 to 36 inches

MAXIMUM ELEVATION: 9,000 feet.

WATER: ⬤ **EXPOSURE:** ☀ ◐

FORM: Habits range from mat-forming to tall, erect, multi-stemmed specimens. Over 200 species.

LANDSCAPE USE: The low, ground-cover varieties work well among pathways and among rocks. The taller varieties are appropriate in beds, mixed borders, among rocks, and as spectacular specimen plants.

PAGE REFERENCE: 108 and 109.

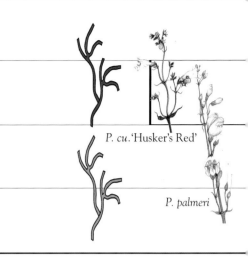

P. cu.'Husker's Red'

P. palmeri

Polygonum aubertii—Silver Lace Vine

Polygonaceae—Buckwheat Family
Deciduous Vine
Height: 25 to 35 feet • Spread: as much as 10 to 15 feet in one season

MAXIMUM ELEVATION: 9,000 feet.

WATER: ⬤ **EXPOSURE:** ☀ ◐

FORM: Intertwining mass of trailing, twisting stems.

LANDSCAPE USE: Good for a summer screen on fences and arbors, particularly in dry locations. Could be used as an informal ground cover. Ideal for covering a chain-link fence.

PAGE REFERENCE: 110.

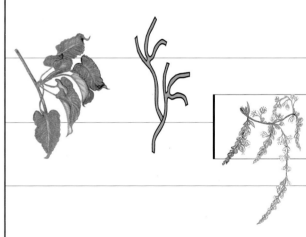

Achillea species—Yarrow

Asteraceae—Sunflower Family
Herbaceous Perennial
Height: 2 inches to 4 feet • Spread: 6 inches to 3 feet

MAXIMUM ELEVATION: 9,000 feet.

WATER: ⬤ **EXPOSURE:** ☀

FORM: Stems are single or loosely clustered either as tall, stately plants or short and matlike.

LANDSCAPE USE: Taller species are appropriate for massed plantings and mixed borders. The lower growing species look great in rock gardens or as a ground cover.

PAGE REFERENCE: 84 and 85.

Alyssoides utriculata—Bladderpod

Brassicaceae—Mustard Family
Herbaceous Perennial
Height: 15 to 24 inches • Spread: 12 inches

MAXIMUM ELEVATION: 8,500 feet.

WATER: 💧   **EXPOSURE:** ☼

FORM: A basal rosette of leaves with flowers growing along the stem.

LANDSCAPE USE: Dry banks, walls, rock gardens, or dry borders. Easily grown for early spring color.

PAGE REFERENCE: 87.

Aurinia saxatile—Basket-of-Gold

Brassicaceae—Mustard Family
Perennial
Height: 6 to 18 inches • Spread: 6 to 12 inches

MAXIMUM ELEVATION: 9,000 feet.

WATER: 💧💧   **EXPOSURE:** ☼

FORM: Loose clumps or hummocks of grayish green leaves. Framework of plant does not dieback like a normal perennial.

LANDSCAPE USE: Effective around rocks as in a rock garden, along walls or bordering a rock pathway. Hard—to—water locations such as steep hillsides. Very showy planted in mass as a ground cover.

PAGE REFERENCE: 90.

Eriogonum umbellatum—Sulphur Flower

Polygonaceae—Buckwheat Family
Perennial Subshrub
Height: 6 to 12 inches • Spread: 1 to 2 feet

MAXIMUM ELEVATION: up to 10,000 feet.

WATER: 💧   **EXPOSURE:** ☼

FORM: Broad loose mats.

LANDSCAPE USE: Ground cover for a dry, sunny flower garden. Well suited for rock gardens and dry banks.

PAGE REFERENCE: 96.

Gaillardia aristata—Blanketflower

Asteraceae—Sunflower Family
Herbaceous Perennial
Height: 2 to 3 feet • Spread: 2 to 3 feet

MAXIMUM ELEVATION: 9,000 feet.

WATER: ⬦ **EXPOSURE:** ☀

FORM: Clump, with erect to spreading stems.

LANDSCAPE USE: Dry meadows, beds, and borders. Plant in groups of 3 or more for impact.

PAGE REFERENCE: 97.

Gutierrezia sarothrae—Snakeweed, Broom Snakeroot, Matchweed, Matchbush, Broomweed, Turpentine Weed

Asteraceae—Sunflower Family
Perennial Subshrub
Height: 12 to 18 inches • Spread: 12 to 18 inches

MAXIMUM ELEVATION: 10,000 feet.

WATER: ⬦ **EXPOSURE:** ☀

FORM: Low and bushy, somewhat woody at the base.

LANDSCAPE USE: Attractive in shortgrass meadows, borders.

PAGE REFERENCE: 98.

Hemerocallis species—Daylily

Liliaceae—Lily Family
Herbaceous Perennial
Height: 1 to 6 feet, (usually about 3½ feet) • Spread: 1 to 3 feet

MAXIMUM ELEVATION: 10,000 feet.

WATER: ⬦⬦ **EXPOSURE:** ☀ ◑

FORM: Large clumps of arching bladelike leaves with flower stems rising above the clump.

LANDSCAPE USE: Versatile. Plant in mass, in mixed borders, on slopes as a tall ground cover, as an informal hedge, or in a cluster as specimen plants.

PAGE REFERENCE: 99.

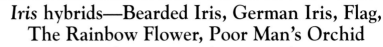

Iris hybrids—Bearded Iris, German Iris, Flag, The Rainbow Flower, Poor Man's Orchid

Iridaceae—Iris Family • Perennial
Height: leaves—1$\frac{1}{2}$ feet tall, flower stems—2 to 3 feet
Spread: 1$\frac{1}{2}$ to 2 feet+

MAXIMUM ELEVATION: 8,500 feet.

WATER: ◌ **EXPOSURE:** ☀

FORM: Clumps of erect swordlike leaves arranged in a fanlike pattern with stems and flowers rising above.

LANDSCAPE USE: An accent along the border or fences and walls, in rock gardens and for early color after spring bulbs have finished.

PAGE REFERENCE: 100 and 101.

Oenothera missouriensis—Ozark Sundrop, Missouri Evening Primrose

Onagraceae—Primrose Family
Herbaceous Perennial
Height: 10 to 12 inches • Spread: 18 to 24 inches

MAXIMUM ELEVATION: 8,000 feet.

WATER: ◌ **EXPOSURE:** ☀

FORM: Prostrate, trailing stems with tips growing upright. Soft, silky appearance.

LANDSCAPE USE: Weaves among other plants, nice rock—garden plant, dry prairie hillsides, part shade, summer ground cover.

PAGE REFERENCE: 105.

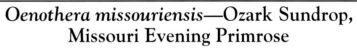

Ratibida columnifera—Prairie Coneflower, Mexican Hat

Asteraceae—Sunflower Family
Herbaceous Perennial
Height: 18 to 24 inches • Spread: 12 to 18 inches

MAXIMUM ELEVATION: 8,000 feet.

WATER: ◌◑ **EXPOSURE:** ☀

FORM: Upright, freely branching from the base, airy clump.

LANDSCAPE USE: Naturalize in grassland planting, cutting garden, herbaceous flower beds.

PAGE REFERENCE: 112.

Stanleya pinnata—Prince's Plume, Golden Prince's Plume, Desert Plume

Brassicaceae—Mustard Family
Perennial Subshrub
Height: 4 to 5 feet • Spread: 2 to 5 feet

MAXIMUM ELEVATION: 8,000 feet.

WATER: ⬤ **EXPOSURE:** ☀

FORM: Woody base with a cluster of coarse leaves producing stout herbaceous stalks, terminating in racemes of spidery, yellow flowers.

LANDSCAPE USE: Naturalized setting, background to perennial bed, foundation planting where water must be held to a minimum.

PAGE REFERENCE: 114.

Tanacetum densum—Partridge Feather

Asteraceae—Sunflower Family
Evergreen Perennial
Height: 6 to 8 inches • Spread: 8 to 12 inches

MAXIMUM ELEVATION: 6,500 feet.

WATER: ⬤ **EXPOSURE:** ☀

FORM: Low mound or mat forming.

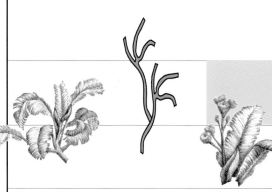

LANDSCAPE USE: Useful in rock gardens, south—facing slopes, dry walls, and banks where silvery white foliage is desired.

PAGE REFERENCE: 115.

Hemerocallis species—Daylily

Liliaceae—Lily Family
Herbaceous Perennial
Height: 1 to 6 feet, (usually about 3½ feet) • Spread: 1 to 3 feet

MAXIMUM ELEVATION: 10,000 feet.

WATER: ⬤⬤ **EXPOSURE:** ☀ ◑

FORM: Large clumps of arching bladelike leaves with flower stems rising above the clump.

LANDSCAPE USE: Versatile. Plant in mass, in mixed borders, on slopes as a tall ground cover, as an informal hedge, or in a cluster as specimen plants.

PAGE REFERENCE: 99.

Asclepias tuberosa—Butterfly Weed, Gay Butterfly, Pleurisy Root, Orange Milkweed

Asclepiadaceae—Milkweed Family
Herbaceous Perennial
Height: 1 to 1¹/₂ feet • Spread: 1 to 2 feet

MAXIMUM ELEVATION: 7,000 feet.

WATER: **EXPOSURE:**

FORM: Erect stems, sometimes sprawling. It is somewhat coarse textured in the landscape. Slow to emerge in spring.

LANDSCAPE USE: Appropriate for very dry, sunny landscapes. Placed in mixed borders, it is especially attractive with blue flowers.

PAGE REFERENCE: 89.

Campsis radicans—Trumpet Vine, Common Trumpet Creeper

Bignoniaceae—Trumpet-creeper Family
Deciduous Vine
Height: 30 feet • Spread: 30 feet, depends on support and structure

MAXIMUM ELEVATION: 5,500 feet.

WATER: **EXPOSURE:**

FORM: Vine climbs via aerial roots that cling to most materials.

LANDSCAPE USE: Covers stone walls, tree trunks and stumps, fences, pergolas, and lath structures. Attracts butterflies.

PAGE REFERENCE: 94 and 95.

Iris hybrids—Bearded Iris, German Iris, Flag, The Rainbow Flower, Poor Man's Orchid

Iridaceae—Iris Family • Perennial
Height: leaves—1¹/₂ feet tall, flower stems—2 to 3 feet
Spread: 1¹/₂ to 2 feet+

MAXIMUM ELEVATION: 8,500 feet.

WATER: **EXPOSURE:**

FORM: Clumps of erect swordlike leaves arranged in a fanlike pattern with stems and flowers rising above.

LANDSCAPE USE: An accent along the border of fences and walls, in rock gardens, and for early color after spring bulbs have finished.

PAGE REFERENCE: 100 and 101.

Agastache cana—Double Bubble Mint, Wild Hyssop, Hummingbird's Mint, Mosquito Plant

Labiatae—Mint Family
Herbaceous Perennial
Height: 2 to 3 feet • Spread: 1¹/₂ to 2 feet

MAXIMUM ELEVATION: 7,500 feet.

WATER: **EXPOSURE:**

FORM: Bushy with branching stems from the ground, narrow leaves along the stems.

LANDSCAPE USE: Very showy perennial for sunny, dry, flower garden.

PAGE REFERENCE: 86.

Centranthus ruber—Red Valerian, Jupiter's Beard, Fox Brush

Valerianaceae—Valerian Family
Herbaceous Perennial
Height: 2 to 3 feet • Spread: 18 to 24 inches

MAXIMUM ELEVATION: 9,000 feet.

WATER: **EXPOSURE:**

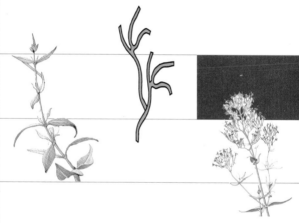

FORM: Bushy clump.

LANDSCAPE USE: Showy plant for low and moderate water zones. Long blooming, attractive perennial for a flower bed.

PAGE REFERENCE: 93.

Gaillardia aristata—Blanketflower

Asteraceae—Sunflower Family
Herbaceous Perennial
Height: 2 to 3 feet • Spread: 2 to 3 feet

MAXIMUM ELEVATION: 9,000 feet.

WATER: **EXPOSURE:**

FORM: Clump, with erect to spreading stems.

LANDSCAPE USE: Dry meadows, beds, and borders. Plant in groups of 3 or more for impact.

PAGE REFERENCE: 97.

Hemerocallis species—Daylily

Liliaceae—Lily Family
Herbaceous Perennial
Height: 1 to 6 feet, (usually about 3¹/₂ feet) • Spread: 1 to 3 feet

MAXIMUM ELEVATION: 10,000 feet.

WATER: **EXPOSURE:**

FORM: Large clumps of arching bladelike leaves with flower stems rising above the clump.

LANDSCAPE USE: Versatile. Plant in mass, in mixed borders, on slopes as a tall ground cover, as an informal hedge, or in a cluster as specimen plants.

PAGE REFERENCE: 99.

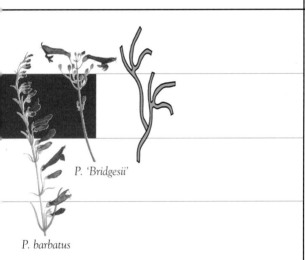

P. 'Bridgesii'

P. barbatus

Penstemon species—Penstemon, Beardtongue

Scroplulariaceae—Snapdragon Family
Herbaceous Perennial
Height: 4 to 48 inches • Spread: 3 to 36 inches

MAXIMUM ELEVATION: 9,000 feet.

WATER: **EXPOSURE:**

FORM: Habits range from mat-forming to tall, erect, multi-stemmed specimens. Over 200 species.

LANDSCAPE USE: The low, ground-cover varieties work well among pathways and among rocks. The taller varieties are appropriate in beds, mixed borders, among rocks, and as spectacular specimen plants.

PAGE REFERENCE: 108 and 109.

Zauschneria arizonica—Hummingbird Trumpet, Arizona Zauschneria

Onagraceae—Evening Primrose Family
Herbaceous Perennial
Height: 12 to 24 inches • Spread: 2 to 4 feet

MAXIMUM ELEVATION: 6,000 feet.

WATER: **EXPOSURE:** ☀

FORM: Erect, upright, thin, narrow-leaved stems with many flowers along the stems, spreading into an airy, compact patch, or colony.

LANDSCAPE USE: Attractive, airy foliage in shortgrass meadow or flower garden; bright red patch of flowers is focal point in the fall landscape.

PAGE REFERENCE: 116.

Achillea species—Yarrow

Asteraceae—Sunflower Family
Herbaceous Perennial
Height: 2 inches to 4 feet • Spread: 6 inches to 3 feet

MAXIMUM ELEVATION: 9,000 feet.

WATER: **EXPOSURE:**

FORM: Stems are single or loosely clustered either as tall, stately plants or short and matlike.

LANDSCAPE USE: Taller species are appropriate for massed plantings and mixed borders. The lower growing species look great in rock gardens or as a ground cover.

PAGE REFERENCE: 84 and 85.

Hemerocallis species—Daylily

Liliaceae—Lily Family
Herbaceous Perennial
Height: 1 to 6 feet, (usually about 3$^{1}/_{2}$ feet) • Spread: 1 to 3 feet

MAXIMUM ELEVATION: 10,000 feet.

WATER: **EXPOSURE:**

FORM: Large clumps of arching bladelike leaves with flower stems rising above the clump.

LANDSCAPE USE: Versatile. Plant in mass, in mixed borders, on slopes as a tall ground cover, as an informal hedge, or in a cluster as specimen plants.

PAGE REFERENCE: 99.

Campanula rotundifolia—Bluebell, Harebell, Bluebells-of-Scotland

Campanulaceae—Bellflower Family
Herbaceous Perennial
Height: 6 to 12 inches first year; older plants up to 24 inches, but lax and sprawling • Spread: 8 inches first year, sprawls

MAXIMUM ELEVATION: 10,000 feet.

WATER: **EXPOSURE:**

FORM: Delicate clumps.

LANDSCAPE USE: Naturalized areas, perennial borders, rock gardens.

PAGE REFERENCE: 92.

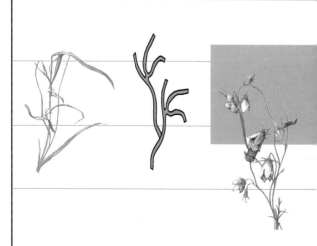

Iris hybrids—Bearded Iris, German Iris, Flag, The Rainbow Flower, Poor Man's Orchid

Iridaceae—Iris Family • Perennial
Height: leaves—1¹/₂ feet tall, flower stems—2 to 3 feet
Spread: 1¹/₂ to 2 feet+

MAXIMUM ELEVATION: 8,500 feet.

WATER: ⬤ **EXPOSURE:** ☀

FORM: Clumps of erect swordlike leaves arranged in a fanlike pattern with stems and flowers rising above.

LANDSCAPE USE: An accent along the border or fences and walls, in rock gardens and for early color after spring bulbs have finished.

PAGE REFERENCE: 100 and 101.

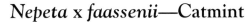

Nepeta x *faassenii*—Catmint

Lamiaceae—Mint Family
Herbaceous Perennial
Height: 18 inches • Spread: 30 inches

MAXIMUM ELEVATION: 6,000 feet.

WATER: ⬤⬤ **EXPOSURE:** ☀ ◐

FORM: Casually mounded.

LANDSCAPE USE: Excellent summertime ground cover. Good for front of dry border or rock garden.

PAGE REFERENCE: 104.

Achillea species—Yarrow

Asteraceae—Sunflower Family
Herbaceous Perennial
Height: 2 inches to 4 feet • Spread: 6 inches to 3 feet

MAXIMUM ELEVATION: 9,000 feet.

WATER: ⬤ **EXPOSURE:** ☀

FORM: Stems are single or loosely clustered either as tall, stately plants or short and matlike.

LANDSCAPE USE: Taller species are appropriate for massed plantings and mixed borders. The lower growing species look great in rock gardens or as a ground cover.

PAGE REFERENCE: 84 and 85.

Iris hybrids—Bearded Iris, German Iris, Flag, The Rainbow Flower, Poor Man's Orchid

Iridaceae—Iris Family • Perennial
Height: leaves—1^1/$_2$ feet tall, flower stems—2 to 3 feet
Spread: 1^1/$_2$ to 2 feet+

MAXIMUM ELEVATION: 8,500 feet.

WATER: ☽ **EXPOSURE:** ☀

FORM: Clumps of erect swordlike leaves arranged in a fanlike pattern with stems and flowers rising above.

LANDSCAPE USE: An accent along the border or fences and walls, in rock gardens and for early color after spring bulbs have finished.

PAGE REFERENCE: 100 and 101.

Liatris punctata—Gayfeather, Dotted Gayfeather, Cachana, Blazing Star

Asteraceae—Sunflower Family
Herbaceous Perennial
Height: 6 to 24 inches • Spread: 12 to 18 inches

MAXIMUM ELEVATION: 8,000 feet.

WATER: ☽ **EXPOSURE:** ☀

FORM: Erect, airy, narrow stems arise from a basal tuft of narrow grass-like leaves.

LANDSCAPE USE: Bank cover among warm season grasses; accent in beds and borders; foundation plantings where water is held to a minimum.

PAGE REFERENCE: 102.

Pulsatilla vulgaris—European Pasqueflower

Ranunculaceae—Buttercup or Crowfoot Family
Herbaceous Perennial
Height: 9 to 12 inches • Spread: 6 to 10 inches

MAXIMUM ELEVATION: 9,500 feet.

WATER: ☽ ☽ **EXPOSURE:** ☀ ☽

FORM: Furry appearance. It is completely covered with hairs.

LANDSCAPE USE: Most often found in rock gardens; most effective in drifts.

PAGE REFERENCE: 111.

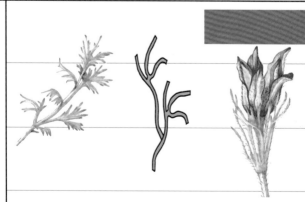

Salvia officinalis—Garden Sage

Lamiaceae—Mint Family
Herbaceous Perennial
Height: 18 to 24 inches • Spread: 12 to 18 inches

MAXIMUM ELEVATION: 9,000 feet.

WATER: **EXPOSURE:**

FORM: Compact, leafy, and shrublike.

LANDSCAPE USE: Perennial mixed borders, planted in mass is very showy, rock gardens, in containers, and as a summertime hedge. Sheared regularly for kitchen use.

PAGE REFERENCE: 113.

Callirhoe involucrata—Wine Cup, Poppy Mallow, Purple Poppy Mallow, Low Poppy Mallow

Malvaceae—Mallow Family
Herbaceous Perennial Ground Cover
Height: 6 to 12 inches • Spread: 1 to 3 feet

MAXIMUM ELEVATION: 6,000 feet.

WATER: **EXPOSURE:**

FORM: Low mat of 1- to 3-foot-long trailing stems.

LANDSCAPE USE: Lovely perennial for sunny dry flower beds (covers nicely around larger plants) and for rock gardens; hangs over walls or along the edge of raised beds.

PAGE REFERENCE: 91.

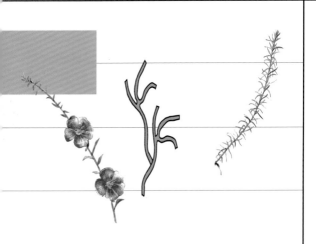

Linum perenne var. lewisii—Blue Flax, Lewis' Flax, Prairie Flax, Perennial Flax

Linaceae—Flax Family
Herbaceous Perennial
Height: 12 to 18 inches • Spread: 12 inches

MAXIMUM ELEVATION: 9,500 feet.

WATER: **EXPOSURE:**

FORM: Erect, airy, vase-shaped.

LANDSCAPE USE: Attractive singly or in groups in informal gardens. Blue flax is short-lived, but self-seeds generously, so is best planted where you can enjoy it moving about from year to year.

PAGE REFERENCE: 103.

Parthenocissus quinquefolia—Virginia Creeper, Woodbine

Vitaceae—Grape Family
Deciduous Vine
Height: 9 inches as ground cover • Spread: 50 to 70 feet

MAXIMUM ELEVATION: 9,000 feet.

WATER: ◯ **EXPOSURE:** ☀ ◐

FORM: Woody trunk and stems form a dense blanket of green foliage.

LANDSCAPE USE: Big, vigorous vine that clings or runs over fence, ground, trellis or brick wall. Can be grown through a small tree; beautiful growing among boulders; good ground cover on slopes.

PAGE REFERENCE: 106.

Penstemon species—Penstemon, Beardtongue

Scroplulariaceae—Snapdragon Family
Herbaceous Perennial
Height: 4 to 48 inches • Spread: 3 to 36 inches

MAXIMUM ELEVATION: 9,000 feet.

WATER: ◯ **EXPOSURE:** ☀ ◐

FORM: Habits range from mat-forming to tall, erect, multi-stemmed specimens. Over 200 species.

LANDSCAPE USE: The low, ground—cover varieties work well among pathways and among rocks. The taller varieties are appropriate in beds, mixed borders, among rocks, and as spectacular specimen plants.

PAGE REFERENCE: 108 and 109.

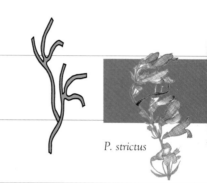

P. strictus

Perovskia atrpliciafolia—Russian Sage

Verbenaceae—Verbena Family
Subscrub Perennial
Height: 3 to 5 feet • Spread: 3 to 4 feet

MAXIMUM ELEVATION: 8,000 feet.

WATER: ◯ **EXPOSURE:** ☀

FORM: Dense, compact, shrublike perennial resembling Salvia.

LANDSCAPE USE: Striking plant for the middle or back of border; useful as a hedge or screen; place in median strips or among other shrubs.

PAGE REFERENCE: 107.

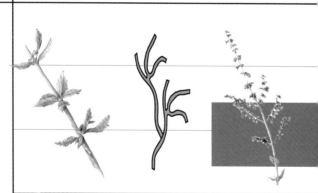

ADDRESS MODULE PLANTING PLAN

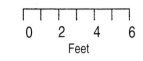

Scale:

0　2　4　6
Feet

North

Plant materials—Address Module

Code	Scientific Name	Common Name	Quantity	Size
1	*Achillea* 'Moonshine,' p. 85 XPG	Moonshine Yarrow	2	1-gal.
2	*Cerastium tomentosum*, p. 124 XPG	Snow-in-Summer	2	Fit-32
3	*Delosperma cooperi*, p. 125 XPG	Purple Hardy Ice Plant	1	Fit-32
4	*Echinacea purpurea*	Purple Coneflower	10	1-gal.
5	*Gaillardia* 'Burgundy,' p. 97 XPG	Burgundy Blanket Flower	4	1-gal.
6	*Leucanthemum* 'Little Miss Muffet'	Little Miss Muffet Daisy	12	1-gal.
7	*Mahonia repens*, p. 165 XPG	Native Creeping Grape Holly	3	1-gal.
8	*Veronica* 'Sunny Border Blue'	Sunny Border Blue Veronica	4	1-gal.

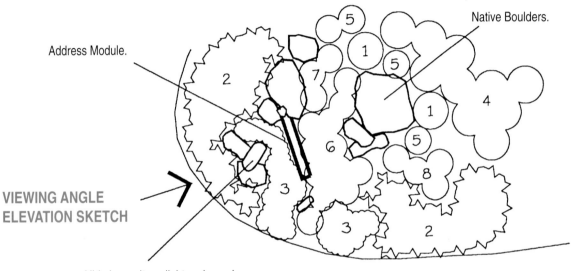

Address Module.

Native Boulders.

VIEWING ANGLE
ELEVATION SKETCH

Hide low-voltage light under rocks.

Driveway

ELEVATION SKETCH—
ADDRESS MODULE DETAIL

Module shall be 6' x 12" x 4' rough sawn timber.
Rout edges to match house timber color.
Stain module to match building trim.
Anchor module with bolts set in concrete.
Numbers shall be 6" brass.

Groundcovers and Grasses

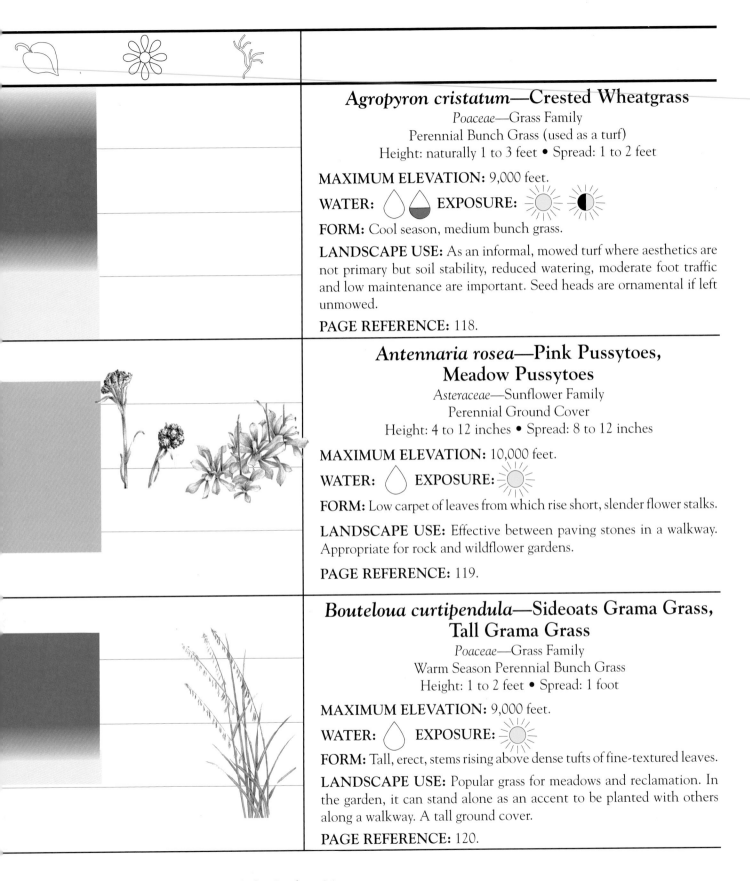

Agropyron cristatum—Crested Wheatgrass

Poaceae—Grass Family
Perennial Bunch Grass (used as a turf)
Height: naturally 1 to 3 feet • Spread: 1 to 2 feet

MAXIMUM ELEVATION: 9,000 feet.

WATER: **EXPOSURE:**

FORM: Cool season, medium bunch grass.

LANDSCAPE USE: As an informal, mowed turf where aesthetics are not primary but soil stability, reduced watering, moderate foot traffic and low maintenance are important. Seed heads are ornamental if left unmowed.

PAGE REFERENCE: 118.

Antennaria rosea—Pink Pussytoes, Meadow Pussytoes

Asteraceae—Sunflower Family
Perennial Ground Cover
Height: 4 to 12 inches • Spread: 8 to 12 inches

MAXIMUM ELEVATION: 10,000 feet.

WATER: **EXPOSURE:**

FORM: Low carpet of leaves from which rise short, slender flower stalks.

LANDSCAPE USE: Effective between paving stones in a walkway. Appropriate for rock and wildflower gardens.

PAGE REFERENCE: 119.

Bouteloua curtipendula—Sideoats Grama Grass, Tall Grama Grass

Poaceae—Grass Family
Warm Season Perennial Bunch Grass
Height: 1 to 2 feet • Spread: 1 foot

MAXIMUM ELEVATION: 9,000 feet.

WATER: **EXPOSURE:**

FORM: Tall, erect, stems rising above dense tufts of fine-textured leaves.

LANDSCAPE USE: Popular grass for meadows and reclamation. In the garden, it can stand alone as an accent to be planted with others along a walkway. A tall ground cover.

PAGE REFERENCE: 120.

Bouteloua gracilis—Blue Grama Grass

Poaceae—Grass Family
Turf Grass or Ornamental Clump Grass
Height: naturally 6 to 24 inches. Mow to 3 inches. • Spread: slowly by weak rhizomes, possibly 2 inches per year.

MAXIMUM ELEVATION: 6,500 feet.

WATER: 💧 **EXPOSURE:** ☀

FORM: Warm season, bunch grass, which becomes more sod-forming when mowed regularly.

LANDSCAPE USE: As a ground cover or lawn on any sunny location not requiring any or very little supplemental irrigation.

PAGE REFERENCE: 121.

Buchloe dactyloides—Buffalograss

Poaceae—Grass Family
Turf Grass
Height: naturally 4 to 8 inches. Mow to 2¹/₂ or 3 inches or leave unmowed. • Spread: by stolons up to 12 inches per year.

MAXIMUM ELEVATION: 6,500 feet.

WATER: 💧 **EXPOSURE:** ☀

FORM: Low growing, warm season, sod forming, dense, smooth textured turf.

LANDSCAPE USE: Wherever an attractive, low-water, low-maintenance turf or ground cover is needed.

PAGE REFERENCE: 122.

Calamagrostis acutiflora—
Karl Foerster Feather Reed Grass

Poaceae—Grass Family
Ornamental Bunch Grass
Height: 3 to 6 feet • Spread: 1 to 2 feet

MAXIMUM ELEVATION: 7,500 feet.

WATER: 💧💧 **EXPOSURE:** ☀

FORM: Cool season, upright and erect with many stems (culms) and leaves forming a dense clump.

LANDSCAPE USE: Let it stand alone as a specimen or in closely planted clusters such as vertical accents in a perennial composition.

PAGE REFERENCE: 123.

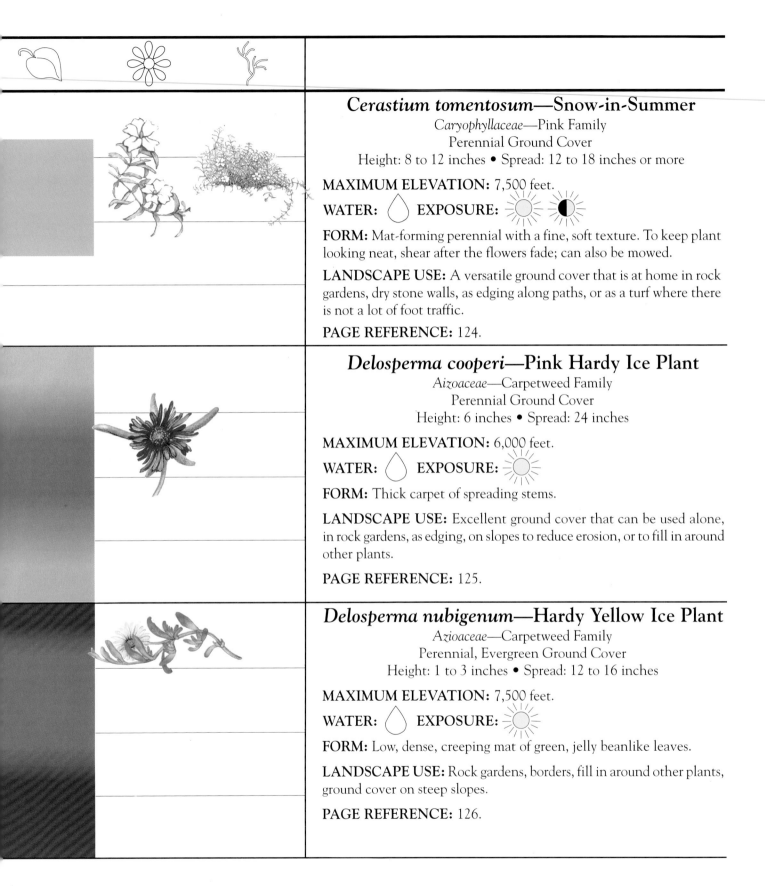

Cerastium tomentosum—Snow-in-Summer

Caryophyllaceae—Pink Family
Perennial Ground Cover
Height: 8 to 12 inches • Spread: 12 to 18 inches or more

MAXIMUM ELEVATION: 7,500 feet.

WATER: **EXPOSURE:**

FORM: Mat-forming perennial with a fine, soft texture. To keep plant looking neat, shear after the flowers fade; can also be mowed.

LANDSCAPE USE: A versatile ground cover that is at home in rock gardens, dry stone walls, as edging along paths, or as a turf where there is not a lot of foot traffic.

PAGE REFERENCE: 124.

Delosperma cooperi—Pink Hardy Ice Plant

Aizoaceae—Carpetweed Family
Perennial Ground Cover
Height: 6 inches • Spread: 24 inches

MAXIMUM ELEVATION: 6,000 feet.

WATER: **EXPOSURE:**

FORM: Thick carpet of spreading stems.

LANDSCAPE USE: Excellent ground cover that can be used alone, in rock gardens, as edging, on slopes to reduce erosion, or to fill in around other plants.

PAGE REFERENCE: 125.

Delosperma nubigenum—Hardy Yellow Ice Plant

Azioaceae—Carpetweed Family
Perennial, Evergreen Ground Cover
Height: 1 to 3 inches • Spread: 12 to 16 inches

MAXIMUM ELEVATION: 7,500 feet.

WATER: **EXPOSURE:**

FORM: Low, dense, creeping mat of green, jelly beanlike leaves.

LANDSCAPE USE: Rock gardens, borders, fill in around other plants, ground cover on steep slopes.

PAGE REFERENCE: 126.

Festuca arundinacea—Tall Fescue

Poaceae—Grass Family
Turf Grass
Height: naturally 1 to 3 feet. Mow to 3 inches. • Spread: 1 to 2 feet

MAXIMUM ELEVATION: 9,000 feet.

WATER: **EXPOSURE:**

FORM: Cool-season, mid-sized bunch grass planted thickly to produce a turf.

LANDSCAPE USE: Anywhere there is a need for a deep green turf and where water conservation is desired.

PAGE REFERENCE: 127.

Festuca ovina glauca—Blue Fescue

Poaceae—Grass Family
Ornamental Perennial Grass
Height: 12 inches • Spread: 12 inches

MAXIMUM ELEVATION: 8,500 feet.

WATER: **EXPOSURE:**

FORM: Fine-textured, compact clumps; does not spread by stolons.

LANDSCAPE USE: Wherever the soft texture and mounded "hummock" shape can provide contrast against other foliage types; in such locations as flower bed borders in rock gardens as an accent plant. Looks particularly attractive in geometric planting patterns.

PAGE REFERENCE: 128.

Helictotrichon sempervirens—Blue Avena Grass, Blue Oat Grass

Poaceae—Grass Family
Ornamental Perennial Grass
Height: 2 to 4 feet in bloom • Spread: 3 feet

MAXIMUM ELEVATION: 8,500 feet.

WATER: **EXPOSURE:**

FORM: Arching, dense, upright clumps or hummocks, similar to Blue Fescue except larger.

LANDSCAPE USE: Architectural interest when used singly or in small groups; provides texture in borders.

PAGE REFERENCE: 129.

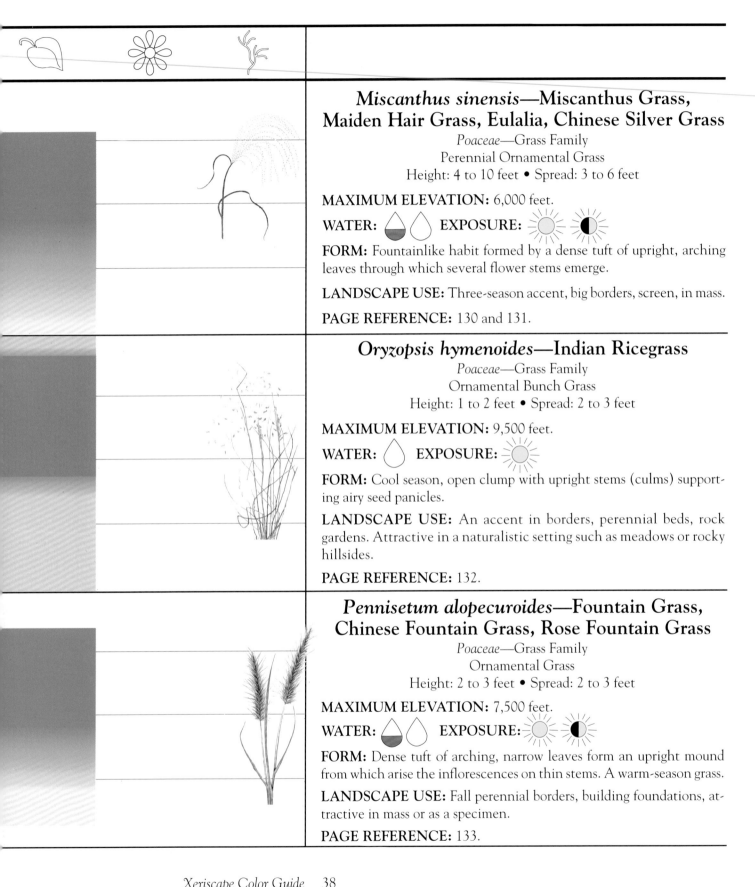

Miscanthus sinensis—Miscanthus Grass, Maiden Hair Grass, Eulalia, Chinese Silver Grass

Poaceae—Grass Family
Perennial Ornamental Grass
Height: 4 to 10 feet • Spread: 3 to 6 feet

MAXIMUM ELEVATION: 6,000 feet.

WATER: **EXPOSURE:**

FORM: Fountainlike habit formed by a dense tuft of upright, arching leaves through which several flower stems emerge.

LANDSCAPE USE: Three-season accent, big borders, screen, in mass.

PAGE REFERENCE: 130 and 131.

Oryzopsis hymenoides—Indian Ricegrass

Poaceae—Grass Family
Ornamental Bunch Grass
Height: 1 to 2 feet • Spread: 2 to 3 feet

MAXIMUM ELEVATION: 9,500 feet.

WATER: **EXPOSURE:**

FORM: Cool season, open clump with upright stems (culms) supporting airy seed panicles.

LANDSCAPE USE: An accent in borders, perennial beds, rock gardens. Attractive in a naturalistic setting such as meadows or rocky hillsides.

PAGE REFERENCE: 132.

Pennisetum alopecuroides—Fountain Grass, Chinese Fountain Grass, Rose Fountain Grass

Poaceae—Grass Family
Ornamental Grass
Height: 2 to 3 feet • Spread: 2 to 3 feet

MAXIMUM ELEVATION: 7,500 feet.

WATER: **EXPOSURE:**

FORM: Dense tuft of arching, narrow leaves form an upright mound from which arise the inflorescences on thin stems. A warm-season grass.

LANDSCAPE USE: Fall perennial borders, building foundations, attractive in mass or as a specimen.

PAGE REFERENCE: 133.

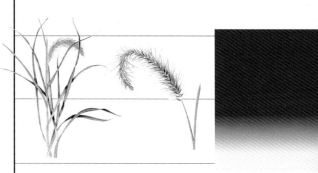

Pennisetum setaceum 'Rubrum'—Purple Fountain Grass or Crimson Fountain Grass

Poaceae—Grass Family
Ornamental Grass
Height: 2 to 4 feet • Spread: 2 to 3 feet

MAXIMUM ELEVATION: 10,000 feet.

WATER: **EXPOSURE:**

FORM: Arching habit; symmetrical mound; soft, featherlike flower plumes.

LANDSCAPE USE: Striking accent along the garden border, mass displays, dried flowers.

PAGE REFERENCE: 134.

Polygonum affine—Himalayan Fleeceflower

Polygonaceae—Buckwheat Family
Perennial Ground Cover (semievergreen)
Height: 6 to 10 inches • Spread: 30 inches or more

MAXIMUM ELEVATION: 8,000 feet.

WATER: **EXPOSURE:**

FORM: Low, trailing mats, a medium texture in the landscape.

LANDSCAPE USE: Borders, rock gardens, ground cover; good soil stabilizer on slopes.

PAGE REFERENCE: 136 and 137.

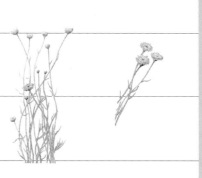

Santolina chamaecyparissus—Lavender Cotton

Asteraceae—Sunflower Family
Subshrub, Evergreen, Ground Cover
Height: 12 to 18 inches • Spread: 12 to 18 inches

MAXIMUM ELEVATION: 8,000 feet.

WATER: **EXPOSURE:**

FORM: Soft-textured mounds.

LANDSCAPE USE: Rock gardens, knot gardens, lower desert landscapes, low hedge, and carpet bedding.

PAGE REFERENCE: 135.

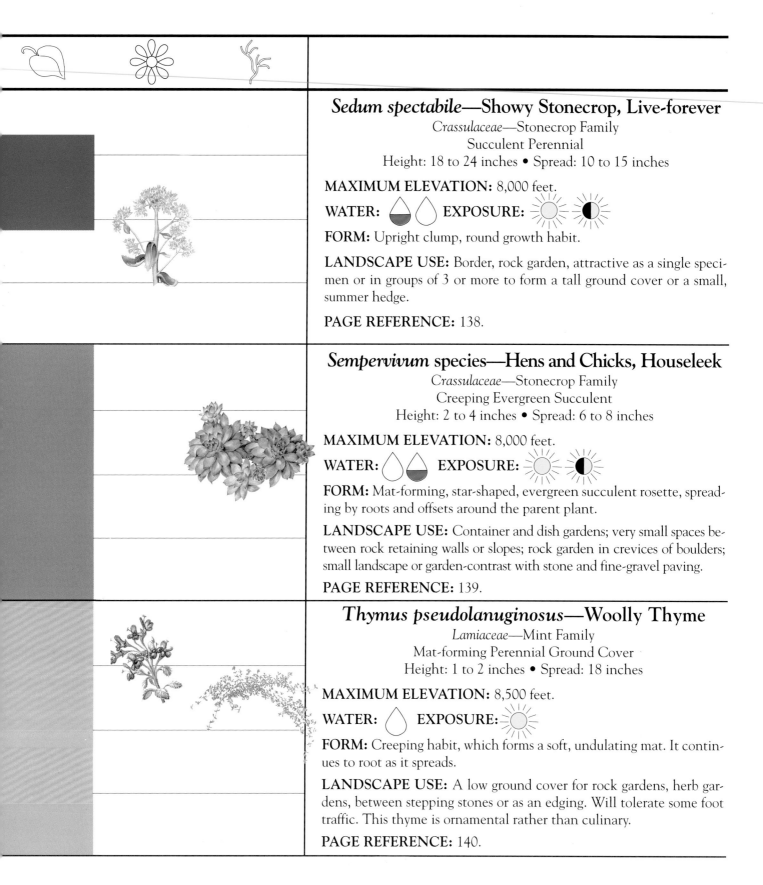

Sedum spectabile—Showy Stonecrop, Live-forever

Crassulaceae—Stonecrop Family
Succulent Perennial
Height: 18 to 24 inches • Spread: 10 to 15 inches

MAXIMUM ELEVATION: 8,000 feet.

WATER: **EXPOSURE:**

FORM: Upright clump, round growth habit.

LANDSCAPE USE: Border, rock garden, attractive as a single specimen or in groups of 3 or more to form a tall ground cover or a small, summer hedge.

PAGE REFERENCE: 138.

Sempervivum species—Hens and Chicks, Houseleek

Crassulaceae—Stonecrop Family
Creeping Evergreen Succulent
Height: 2 to 4 inches • Spread: 6 to 8 inches

MAXIMUM ELEVATION: 8,000 feet.

WATER: **EXPOSURE:**

FORM: Mat-forming, star-shaped, evergreen succulent rosette, spreading by roots and offsets around the parent plant.

LANDSCAPE USE: Container and dish gardens; very small spaces between rock retaining walls or slopes; rock garden in crevices of boulders; small landscape or garden-contrast with stone and fine-gravel paving.

PAGE REFERENCE: 139.

Thymus pseudolanuginosus—Woolly Thyme

Lamiaceae—Mint Family
Mat-forming Perennial Ground Cover
Height: 1 to 2 inches • Spread: 18 inches

MAXIMUM ELEVATION: 8,500 feet.

WATER: **EXPOSURE:**

FORM: Creeping habit, which forms a soft, undulating mat. It continues to root as it spreads.

LANDSCAPE USE: A low ground cover for rock gardens, herb gardens, between stepping stones or as an edging. Will tolerate some foot traffic. This thyme is ornamental rather than culinary.

PAGE REFERENCE: 140.

Veronica pectinata—Blue Woolly Speedwell

Scrophulariaceae—Figwort Family
Mat-forming perennial Ground Cover
Height: 1 to 2 inches • Spread: 12 to 18 inches

MAXIMUM ELEVATION: 8,500 feet.

WATER: **EXPOSURE:**

FORM: Ground-hugging mat.

LANDSCAPE USE: Exceptionally attractive ground cover for full sun or light shade. Especially nice between stepping stones or where allowed to cascade over a wall.

PAGE REFERENCE: 141.

Zinnia grandiflora—Paper Flower, Desert Zinnia, Rocky Mountain Zinnia

Asteraceae—Sunflower Family
Ground Cover or Subshrub
Height: 6 to 8 inches • Spread: 10 inches or more

MAXIMUM ELEVATION: 6,000 feet.

WATER: **EXPOSURE:**

FORM: Lacy, compact mound.

LANDSCAPE USE: Effective when allowed to develop into large patches. Use for dense ground cover, low borders, and shortgrass meadows.

PAGE REFERENCE: 142.

PLANTING PLAN—NARROW TREE LAWN

Scale:
0 2 4 6

North

Sidewalk

Street

(2) *Acer ginnala* 'Flame'
2.5"—Cal.
p. 3 XPG

The plan may be mirrored for this side of the access walk. If mirrored, double the plant material quantities.

(100) *Cerastium tomentosum*—Snow-in-Summer 1-Gal. (an option is to plant 3 flats of 32 to save cost).

(10) *Schizachyrium scoparium*—Little Blue Stem 1-Gal.

SHADE PLANTING BEDS

Place large, smooth river boulders.
Set boulders down into the ground for
natural appearance.
Place topsoil around boulders.
Place boulders with relative sizes as
shown. The largest being 3 tons, the
smallest being 500 pounds.

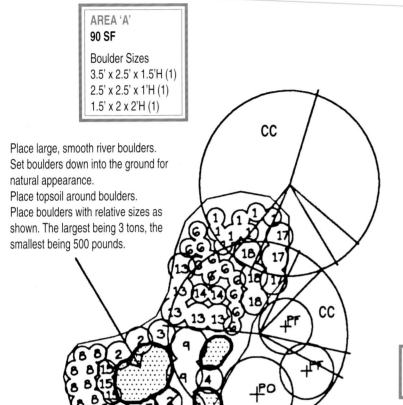

Irrigation Notes:
It is recommended that a hose end irrigation system be used.
Irrigate all plantings through the establishment period for
each. Watering frequency may be less depending on rainfall.
Perennials-first growing season.
Irrigate at the first sign of drought stress and then to about the
depth of root mass.
Shrubs-Twice monthly for the first growing season.
Trees-monthly for three to four growing seasons.
Foliar feed each three weeks for the first growing season.

Planting Notes:
Backfill planting pits with a 50/50 compost/topsoil mix. Set all
trees plumb. Stake all trees with two steel 'T' posts, nylon
straps, and 10 ga. wire. Place Fir Fiber Mulch 2 inches deep
around the base of all newly planted trees and shrubs, and
perennial planting areas.
Place a 3-inch high irrigation ring around all trees and shrubs.

AREA 'B'
40 SF

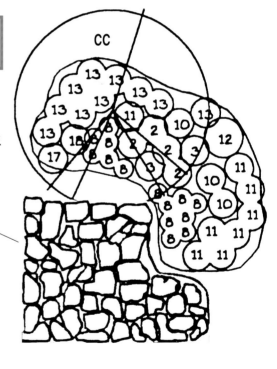

'Thunder River Buff' stepping stone patio
Miniumum stone size 1 SF • maximum 3 SF.
Set stones on sand bed.
Space stones approx. 1.5 inches apart.
Fill spaces with sand topsoil mix.
190 SF of stones required.

Plant Materials—Perennials

Code	Scientific Name	Common Name	Quantity	Size
1	Achillea lanulosa	Native White Yarrow (N)	8	1-gal.
2	Aquilegia caerulea	Rocky Mountain Columbine (N)	7	1-gal.
3	Aquilegia elegantuia	Native Red Columbine (N)	2	1-gal.
4	Atemeala frigida	Fringed Sage (N)	1	1-gal.
6	Aster porteri	Porter's Aster (N)	11	1-gal.
7	Campanula rotundifolia, p. 91 XPG	Harebell (N)	3	1-gal.
8	Cerestium tomentosum, p. 124 XPG	Snow-in-Summer	27	1-gal.
9	Chemerion angustifolium	Fireweed (N)	3	1-gal.
10	Delphineum grandifolum 'Butterfly'	Butterfly Delphineum	3	1-gal.
11	Erigeron compositus	Fern-leaf Fleabane (N)	8	1-gal.
12	Helenium hoopesii	Orange Helen's Flower (N)	1	1-gal.
13	Leucanthemum 'Little Miss Muffet'	Dwarf Shasta Daisy	15	1-gal.
14	Lupinus 'Gallery Red'	Gallery Red Lupine	2	1-gal.
15	Mahonia repens, p. 165 XPG	Creeping Grape Holly (N)	3	1-gal.
16	Papaver nudicale	Iceland Poppy	2	1-gal.
17	Penstemon alphus, p. 108 XPG	Alpha Penstemon	4	1-gal.
18	Penstemon strictus, p. 108 XPG	Rocky Mountain Penstemon (N)	4	1-gal.
		Total	**104**	**1-gal.**

Plant Materials—Shrubs

Code	Scientific Name	Common Name	Quantity	Size
PO	Physocarpus opulfolius 'Nanus'	Dwarf Ninebark (N)	1	5-gal.
PF	Potentilla fruiticosa, p. 54 XPG	Bush Cinquifoil (N)	2	5-gal.
CC	Crataegus crus-galli, p. 32 XPG	Cockspur Hawthorn	3	5-gal.
		Total	**6**	**5-gal.**

NORTH

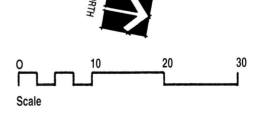

0   10   20   30

Scale

Annuals

Gomphrena globosa—Globe Amaranth

Amaranthaceae—Amaranth Family
Tender Annual
Height: 10 to 20 inches • Spread: 10 to 20 inches

MAXIMUM ELEVATION: 10,000 feet.

WATER: 🌢🌢 **EXPOSURE:** ☀

FORM: Dense mat of leaves from which rise erect, long, slender flower stems.

LANDSCAPE USE: Containers, borders, and beddings.

PAGE REFERENCE: 147.

Portulaca grandiflora—Moss Rose, Rose Moss, Portulaca

Portulacaceae—Purslane Family
Tender Annual, Ground Cover
Height: 4 to 6 inches • Spread: 10 inches

MAXIMUM ELEVATION: 10,000 feet.

WATER: 🌢 **EXPOSURE:** ☀

FORM: Low growing, trailing succulent.

LANDSCAPE USE: Best used in hot, dry, sunny areas. Good for rock gardens, edging, dry slopes, containers, and between rocks in walls and open spaces between stepping stones.

PAGE REFERENCE: 149.

Coreopsis tinctoria—Tickseed, Calliopsis, Golden Coreopsis

Asteraceae—Sunflower Family
Half-hardy Annual
Height: 18 to 40 inches • Spread: 4 to 8 inches

MAXIMUM ELEVATION: 10,000 feet.

WATER: 🌢 **EXPOSURE:** ☀

FORM: Wispy stems support large flowers. When planted in mass, are very attractive and easily swayed by the wind.

LANDSCAPE USE: Good for naturalizing and is appropriate in more formal settings such as borders, edging, and mixed annual-perennial beds.

PAGE REFERENCE: 144.

Cosmos sulphureus—Yellow Cosmos

Asteraceae—Sunflower Family
Tender Annual
Height: 2 to 4 feet • Spread: single, wiry stem will have leaves and
stems that spread approximately 6 to 12 inches

MAXIMUM ELEVATION: 10,000 feet.

WATER: **EXPOSURE:**

FORM: Tall, open and branching, airy texture.

LANDSCAPE USE: Sunny flower beds and cottage gardens, meadows (perennial grasses will crowd Cosmos out after several years), open
areas of a lawn.

PAGE REFERENCE: 145.

Gomphrena globosa—Globe Amaranth

Amaranthaceae—Amaranth Family
Tender Annual
Height: 10 to 20 inches • Spread: 10 to 20 inches

MAXIMUM ELEVATION: 10,000 feet.

WATER: **EXPOSURE:**

FORM: Dense mat of leaves from which rise erect, long, slender flower
stems.

LANDSCAPE USE: Containers, borders, and beddings.

PAGE REFERENCE: 147.

Portulaca grandiflora—Moss Rose, Rose Moss, Portulaca

Portulacaceae—Purslane Family
Tender Annual, Ground Cover
Height: 4 to 6 inches • Spread: 10 inches

MAXIMUM ELEVATION: 10,000 feet.

WATER: **EXPOSURE:**

FORM: Low growing, trailing succulent.

LANDSCAPE USE: Best used in hot, dry, sunny areas. Good for rock
gardens, edging, dry slopes, containers, and between rocks in walls and
open spaces between stepping stones.

PAGE REFERENCE: 149.

Sanvitalia procumbens—Creeping Zinnia
Asteraceae—Sunflower Family
Half-hardy Annual
Height: 4 to 6 inches • Spread: trails 12 to 16 inches
(space 4 to 6 inches apart)

MAXIMUM ELEVATION: 10,000 feet.

WATER: **EXPOSURE:**

FORM: Trailing, spreading mats.

LANDSCAPE USE: Edging, bedding, ground cover, rock gardens, walls, hanging baskets, and steep banks.

PAGE REFERENCE: 151.

Tropaeolum majus 'Alaska'—Nasturtium
Tropaeolaceae—Nasturtium Family
Tender Annual
Height: 6 to 12 inches • Spread: 10 to 15 inches

MAXIMUM ELEVATION: 10,000 feet.

WATER: **EXPOSURE:**

FORM: Dense, compact, and bushy.

LANDSCAPE USE: Beds, hanging over walls, containers, hanging baskets.

PAGE REFERENCE: 152.

Zinnia augustifolia—Narrowleaf Zinnia
Asteraceae—Sunflower Family
Annual
Height: 12 to 18 inches • Spread: 12 to 18 inches

MAXIMUM ELEVATION: 10,000 feet.

WATER: **EXPOSURE:**

FORM: Trailing stems form a compact mound.

LANDSCAPE USE: Containers, window boxes, beds, borders, summer ground cover.

PAGE REFERENCE: 153.

Coreopsis tinctoria—Tickseed, Calliopsis, Golden Coreopsis

Asteraceae—Sunflower Family
Half-hardy Annual
Height: 18 to 40 inches • Spread: 4 to 8 inches

MAXIMUM ELEVATION: 10,000 feet.

WATER: ◇ **EXPOSURE:** ☼

FORM: Wispy stems support large flowers. When planted in mass, are very attractive and easily swayed by the wind.

LANDSCAPE USE: Good for naturalizing and is appropriate in more formal settings such as borders, edging, and mixed annual-perennial beds.

PAGE REFERENCE: 144.

Eschscholzia californica—California Poppy

Papaveraceae—Poppy Family
Hardy Annual or Short-lived Perennial
Height: 12 inches • Spread: 12 inches

MAXIMUM ELEVATION: 9,000 feet.

WATER: ◇ **EXPOSURE:** ☼ ◐

FORM: Casually rounded.

LANDSCAPE USE: Good for naturalizing in wild gardens, also useful in beds, borders, and containers.

PAGE REFERENCE: 146.

Gomphrena globosa—Globe Amaranth

Amaranthaceae—Amaranth Family
Tender Annual
Height: 10 to 20 inches • Spread: 10 to 20 inches

MAXIMUM ELEVATION: 10,000 feet.

WATER: ◖ ◇ **EXPOSURE:** ☼

FORM: Dense mat of leaves from which rise erect, long, slender flower stems.

LANDSCAPE USE: Containers, borders, and beddings.

PAGE REFERENCE: 147.

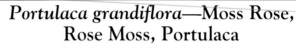

Portulaca grandiflora—Moss Rose, Rose Moss, Portulaca

Portulacaceae—Purslane Family
Tender Annual, Ground Cover
Height: 4 to 6 inches • Spread: 10 inches

MAXIMUM ELEVATION: 10,000 feet.

WATER: ○ **EXPOSURE:** ☀

FORM: Low growing, trailing succulent.

LANDSCAPE USE: Best used in hot, dry, sunny areas. Good for rock gardens, edging, dry slopes, containers, and between rocks in walls and open spaces between stepping stones.

PAGE REFERENCE: 149.

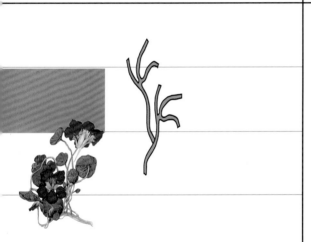

Tropaeolum majus 'Alaska'—Nasturtium

Tropaeolaceae—Nasturtium Family
Tender Annual
Height: 6 to 12 inches • Spread: 10 to 15 inches

MAXIMUM ELEVATION: 10,000 feet.

WATER: ● ○ **EXPOSURE:**

FORM: Dense, compact, and bushy.

LANDSCAPE USE: Beds, hanging over walls, containers, hanging baskets.

PAGE REFERENCE: 152.

Cosmos bipinnatus—Cosmos, Mexican Aster

Asteraceae—Sunflower Family
Tender Annual
Height: 2 to 4 feet • Spread: single, wiry stem will have leaves and stems that spread approximately 6 to 12 inches

MAXIMUM ELEVATION: 10,000 feet.

WATER: ○ **EXPOSURE:** ☀

FORM: Tall, open and branching, airy texture.

LANDSCAPE USE: Sunny flower beds and cottage gardens, meadows (perennial grasses will crowd Cosmos out after several years), open areas of a lawn.

PAGE REFERENCE: 145.

Gomphrena globosa—Globe Amaranth
Amaranthaceae—Amaranth Family
Tender Annual
Height: 10 to 20 inches • Spread: 10 to 20 inches

MAXIMUM ELEVATION: 10,000 feet.

WATER: **EXPOSURE:**

FORM: Dense mat of leaves from which rise erect, long, slender flower stems.

LANDSCAPE USE: Containers, borders, and beddings.

PAGE REFERENCE: 147.

Portulaca grandiflora—Moss Rose, Rose Moss, Portulaca
Portulacaceae—Purslane Family
Tender Annual, Ground Cover
Height: 4 to 6 inches • Spread: 10 inches

MAXIMUM ELEVATION: 10,000 feet.

WATER: **EXPOSURE:**

FORM: Low growing, trailing succulent.

LANDSCAPE USE: Best used in hot, dry, sunny areas. Good for rock gardens, edging, dry slopes, containers, and between rocks in walls and open spaces between stepping stones.

PAGE REFERENCE: 149.

Tropaeolum majus 'Alaska'—Nasturtium
Tropaeolaceae—Nasturtium Family
Tender Annual
Height: 6 to 12 inches • Spread: 10 to 15 inches

MAXIMUM ELEVATION: 10,000 feet.

WATER: **EXPOSURE:**

FORM: Dense, compact, and bushy.

LANDSCAPE USE: Beds, hanging over walls, containers, hanging baskets.

PAGE REFERENCE: 152.

Coreopsis tinctoria—Tickseed, Calliopsis, Golden Coreopsis

Asteraceae—Sunflower Family
Half-hardy Annual
Height: 18 to 40 inches • Spread: 4 to 8 inches

MAXIMUM ELEVATION: 10,000 feet.

WATER: **EXPOSURE:**

FORM: Wispy stems support large flowers. When planted in mass, are very attractive and easily swayed by the wind.

LANDSCAPE USE: Good for naturalizing and is appropriate in more formal settings such as borders, edging, and mixed annual-perennial beds.

PAGE REFERENCE: 144.

Tropaeolum majus 'Alaska'—Nasturtium

Tropaeolaceae—Nasturtium Family
Tender Annual
Height: 6 to 12 inches • Spread: 10 to 15 inches

MAXIMUM ELEVATION: 10,000 feet.

WATER: **EXPOSURE:**

FORM: Dense, compact, and bushy.

LANDSCAPE USE: Beds, hanging over walls, containers, hanging baskets.

PAGE REFERENCE: 152.

Cosmos bipinnatus—Cosmos, Mexican Aster

Asteraceae—Sunflower Family
Tender Annual
Height: 2 to 4 feet • Spread: single, wiry stem will have leaves and stems that spread approximately 6 to 12 inches

MAXIMUM ELEVATION: 10,000 feet.

WATER: **EXPOSURE:**

FORM: Tall, open and branching, airy texture.

LANDSCAPE USE: Sunny flower beds and cottage gardens, meadows (perennial grasses will crowd Cosmos out after several years), open areas of a lawn.

PAGE REFERENCE: 145.

Gomphrena globosa—Globe Amaranth

Amaranthaceae—Amaranth Family
Tender Annual
Height: 10 to 20 inches • Spread: 10 to 20 inches

MAXIMUM ELEVATION: 10,000 feet.

WATER: ◓ ◯ **EXPOSURE:** ☀

FORM: Dense mat of leaves from which rise erect, long, slender flower stems.

LANDSCAPE USE: Containers, borders, and beddings.

PAGE REFERENCE: 147.

Lavatera trimestris—Annual Mallow

Malvaceae—Mallow Family
Hardy Annual
Height: 2 to 4 feet • Spread: space 18 to 24 inches apart

MAXIMUM ELEVATION: 10,000 feet.

WATER: ◓ ◯ **EXPOSURE:** ☀

FORM: Dense, bushy mound.

LANDSCAPE USE: Middle or rear of sunny, mixed border; colorful, fast growing, low, summer hedge.

PAGE REFERENCE: 148.

Cosmos bipinnatus—Cosmos, Mexican Aster

Asteraceae—Sunflower Family
Tender Annual
Height: 2 to 4 feet • Spread: single, wiry stem will have leaves and stems that spread approximately 6 to 12 inches

MAXIMUM ELEVATION: 10,000 feet.

WATER: ◯ **EXPOSURE:** ☀

FORM: Tall, open and branching, airy texture.

LANDSCAPE USE: Sunny flower beds and cottage gardens, meadows (perennial grasses will crowd Cosmos out after several years), open areas of a lawn.

PAGE REFERENCE: 145.

Gomphrena globosa—Globe Amaranth

Amaranthaceae—Amaranth Family
Tender Annual
Height: 10 to 20 inches • Spread: 10 to 20 inches

MAXIMUM ELEVATION: 10,000 feet.

WATER: 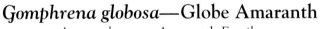 **EXPOSURE:**

FORM: Dense mat of leaves from which rise erect, long, slender flower stems.

LANDSCAPE USE: Containers, borders, and beddings.

PAGE REFERENCE: 147.

Coreopsis tinctoria—Tickseed, Calliopsis, Golden Coreopsis

Asteraceae—Sunflower Family
Half-hardy Annual
Height: 18 to 40 inches • Spread: 4 to 8 inches

MAXIMUM ELEVATION: 10,000 feet.

WATER: **EXPOSURE:**

FORM: Wispy stems support large flowers. When planted in mass, are very attractive and easily swayed by the wind.

LANDSCAPE USE: Good for naturalizing and is appropriate in more formal settings such as borders, edging, and mixed annual-perennial beds.

PAGE REFERENCE: 144.

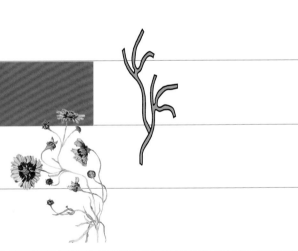

Gomphrena globosa—Globe Amaranth

Amaranthaceae—Amaranth Family
Tender Annual
Height: 10 to 20 inches • Spread: 10 to 20 inches

MAXIMUM ELEVATION: 10,000 feet.

WATER: **EXPOSURE:**

FORM: Dense mat of leaves from which rise erect, long, slender flower stems.

LANDSCAPE USE: Containers, borders, and beddings.

PAGE REFERENCE: 147.

Salvia sclarea—Clary Sage

Lamiaceae—Mint Family
Biennial Herb
Height: 3 feet • Spread: 1 to 2 feet

MAXIMUM ELEVATION: 7,500 feet.

WATER: ◇ **EXPOSURE:** ☼ ☽

FORM: Herbaceous, large rosette of basal leaves with rigid spikes of showy flowers above.

LANDSCAPE USE: Splendid background for lower growing annuals and perennials. Use in mixed borders or clustered together for a large display. Appropriate for the herb garden, too.

PAGE REFERENCE: 150.

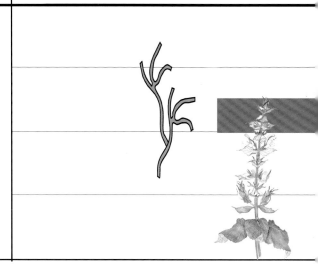

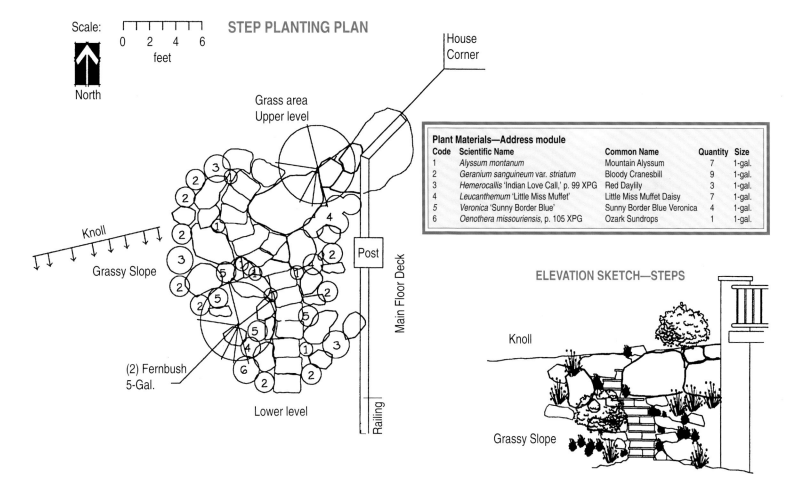

Scale: 0 2 4 6 feet

North

STEP PLANTING PLAN

Grass area
Upper level

House Corner

Knoll

Grassy Slope

Post

Main Floor Deck

Railing

(2) Fernbush
5-Gal.

Lower level

Plant Materials—Address module				
Code	Scientific Name	Common Name	Quantity	Size
1	*Alyssum montanum*	Mountain Alyssum	7	1-gal.
2	*Geranium sanguineum var. striatum*	Bloody Cranesbill	9	1-gal.
3	*Hemerocallis* 'Indian Love Call,' p. 99 XPG	Red Daylily	3	1-gal.
4	*Leucanthemum* 'Little Miss Muffet'	Little Miss Muffet Daisy	7	1-gal.
5	*Veronica* 'Sunny Border Blue'	Sunny Border Blue Veronica	4	1-gal.
6	*Oenothera missouriensis*, p. 105 XPG	Ozark Sundrops	1	1-gal.

ELEVATION SKETCH—STEPS

Knoll

Grassy Slope

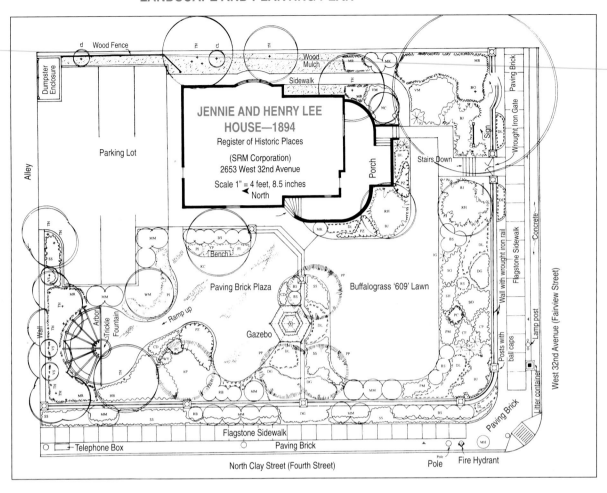

JENNIE AND HENRY LEE
HOUSE—1894

Register of Historic Places

(SRM Corporation)
2653 West 32nd Avenue

Scale 1" = 4 feet, 8.5 inches
North

Code	Scientific Name	Common Name
Plant Materials—Trees		
TH	*Ailanthus altissima*	Tree of Heaven (existing)
AP	*Pinus nigra*	Austrian Pine
PP	*Pinus ponderosa*, p. 53 XPG	Ponderosa Pine
RH	*Craetaegus ambigua*	Russian Hawthorn
KC	*Gymnocladus dioicus*, p. 40 XPG	Kentucky Coffeetree
BO	*Quercus macrocarpa*, p. 64 XPG	Burr Oak
Plant Materials—Shrubs		
MM	*Cercocarpus ledifolius*, p. 22 XPG	Mountain Mahogany
RB	*Chrysothamnus sp.*, p. 26 XPG	Rabbitbrush
BJ	*Juniperus sabina* 'Buffalo'	Buffalo Juniper
VS	*Spirea x Vanhoutte*, p. 74 XPG	Vanhoutte Spirea (existing)
MK	*Syringa panula* 'Miss Kim'	Miss Kim Lilac
CL	*Syringa vulgaris*, p. 76 XPG	Common Lilac (existing)
BS	*Caryopteris incana*	Blue Mist Spirea
NC	*Prunus tomentosa*	Nanking Cherry
WM	*Acer grandidentatum*, p. 4 XPG	Wasatch Maple
Plant Materials—Perennials		
DL	*Hemerocallis* (mixed), p.99 XPG	Daylily
RS	*Perovskia atriplicifolia*, p. 107 XPG	Russian Sage
PC	*Echinacea purpurea*	Purple Coneflower
WY	*Achillea millefolium lanulosa*, p. 85 XPG	White Yarrow
PM	*Callirhoe involucrata*, p. 91 XPG	Poppy Mallow

Code	Scientific Name	Common Name
Plant Materials—Perennials, cont.		
BD	*Melampodium leucanthum*	Blackfoot Daisy
CF	*Berlandiera lyrata*	Chocolate Flower
PZ	*Zinnia grandiflora*, p. 142 XPG	Prairie Zinnia
PI	*Delosperma cooperi*, p. 125 XPG	Purple Iceplant
DG	*Gaillardia aristata* 'Goblin,' p. 97 XPG	Dwarf Blanket Flower
CP	*Ratibida columnifera*, p. 112 XPG	Prairie Coneflower
SH	*Stachys coccinea*	Scarlet Hedgenettle
SG	*Viguiera multiflora*	Showy Goldeneye
CD	*Erigeron compositus*	Cut Leaf Daisy
Plant Materials—Groundcovers		
HB	*Polygonum affine*, p. 136 XPG	Himalayan Border Jewel
MR	*Mahonia repens*, p. 165 XPG	Creeping Mahonia
SS	*Cerastium tomentosum*, p. 124 XPG	Snow-in-Summer
VM	*Vinca Minor* 'Bowles'	Periwinkle
YP	*Delosperma nubigenum*, p. 126 XPG	Yellow Hardy Ice Plant
Plant Materials—Grasses		
IG	*Sorghastrum nutans*	Indiangrass
BG	*Buchloe dactyloides* '609', p. 122 XPG	Buffalograss
Plant Materials—Annuals		
	Mass or mix for effect	

A Contemporary
Victorian Garden

A Xeriscape Design
by Ken Ball, Denver Water

Shade Plants

Arctostaphylos uva-ursi—Kinnikinnick, Bearberry

Ericaceae—Heath Family
Broadleaf Evergreen Shrub
Height: 3 to 6 inches • Spread: 24 to 36 inches

MAXIMUM ELEVATION: 10,000 feet.

WATER: **EXPOSURE:**

FORM: Prostrate, trailing, mat-forming.

LANDSCAPE USE: Evergreen ground cover particularly in rocky sites; wildlife gardens; naturalizing under trees or in rock gardens.

PAGE REFERENCE: 157.

Philadelphus microphyllus— Littleleaf Mockorange

Saxifragaceae—Saxifrage Family
Deciduous Shrub
Height: 4 to 6 feet • Spread: 4 to 6 feet

MAXIMUM ELEVATION: 8,000 feet.

WATER: **EXPOSURE:**

FORM: Upright, tight, compact, and rounded.

LANDSCAPE USE: This shrub is primarily of interest to native plant enthusiasts but has value wherever a small deciduous shrub is needed. Splendid in perennial border or rock garden.

PAGE REFERENCE: 166.

Ptelea trifoliata—Hop Tree, Wafer Ash, Stinking Ash

Rutaceae—Rue Family
Large Shrub or Small Tree
Height: 15 to 20 feet • Spread: 15 to 20 feet

MAXIMUM ELEVATION: 9,000 feet.

WATER: **EXPOSURE:**

FORM: A few strong leaders support open branching and foliage, making a tall, rounded shrub, or if pruned to one leader, an attractive, narrow, small tree results.

LANDSCAPE USE: Hedge, specimen, ideal tree for a small landscape.

PAGE REFERENCE: 168 and 169.

Ribes aureum—Golden Currant

Grossulariaceae—Currant or Gooseberry Family
Deciduous Shrub
Height: 4 to 6 feet • Spread: 4 to 6 feet

MAXIMUM ELEVATION: 10,000 feet.

WATER: **EXPOSURE:**

FORM: Erect, open, multi-stemmed, deciduous shrub. Forms a clump. If browsed or clipped, twigs and foliage will increase in density.

LANDSCAPE USE: Wildlife plantings, fruit gardens, low shelterbelts, background plants; ornamental use wherever an open shrubby clump is desired.

PAGE REFERENCE: 170 and 171.

Rosa glauca or *Rosa rubrifolia*—Redleaf Rose

Rosaceae—Rose Family
Deciduous Shrub
Height: 6 to 7 feet • Spread: 4 to 6 feet

MAXIMUM ELEVATION: 8,500 feet.

WATER: **EXPOSURE:**

FORM: Upright, fairly open, arching branches, medium texture.

LANDSCAPE USE: Barrier plantings, background to perennial beds, mixed shrub borders, mixed perennial borders, and as specimen plants.

PAGE REFERENCE: 167.

Rubus deliciosus—Boulder Raspberry, Thimbleberry

Rosaceae—Rose Family
Deciduous Shrub
Height: 4 to 6 feet • Spread: 5 to 8 feet

MAXIMUM ELEVATION: 9,000 feet.

WATER: **EXPOSURE:**

FORM: Arching branches form a loose, vase-shaped shrub.

LANDSCAPE USE: A very attractive shrub that does well in dry shade. Use in mass groupings, to attract birds, and for naturalizing.

PAGE REFERENCE: 172 and 173.

Symphoricarpos x chenaultii— Chenault Coralberry

Caprifoliaceae—Honeysuckle Family
Deciduous Shrub
Height: 3 to 4 feet • Spread: 3 to 6 feet

MAXIMUM ELEVATION: 7,500 feet.

WATER: **EXPOSURE:**

FORM: Narrow, upright, arching branches spread to the ground, creating a loose, sprawling mound.

LANDSCAPE USE: Mass grouping on a steep bank; naturalizing.

PAGE REFERENCE: 176.

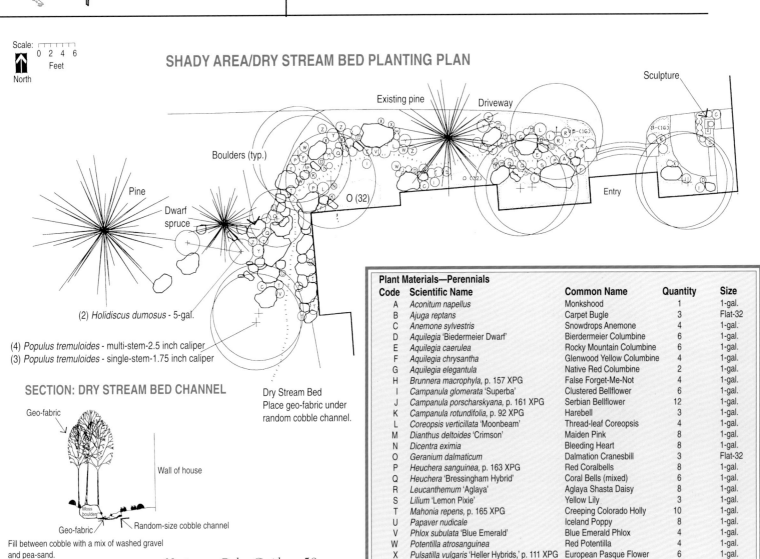

Scale:
0 2 4 6
Feet
North

SHADY AREA/DRY STREAM BED PLANTING PLAN

Existing pine
Driveway
Sculpture
Boulders (typ.)
Pine
Dwarf spruce
O (32)
Entry

(2) *Holidiscus dumosus* - 5-gal.

(4) *Populus tremuloides* - multi-stem-2.5 inch caliper
(3) *Populus tremuloides* - single-stem-1.75 inch caliper

SECTION: DRY STREAM BED CHANNEL

Geo-fabric
Wall of house
Moss boulder
Geo-fabric
Random-size cobble channel

Fill between cobble with a mix of washed gravel and pea-sand.

Dry Stream Bed
Place geo-fabric under random cobble channel.

Xeriscape Color Guide 58

Plant Materials—Perennials			
Code	Scientific Name	Common Name	Quantity	Size
A	*Aconitum napellus*	Monkshood	1	1-gal.
B	*Ajuga reptans*	Carpet Bugle	3	Flat-32
C	*Anemone sylvestris*	Snowdrops Anemone	4	1-gal.
D	*Aquilegia* 'Biedermeier Dwarf'	Bierdermeier Columbine	6	1-gal.
E	*Aquilegia caerulea*	Rocky Mountain Columbine	6	1-gal.
F	*Aquilegia chrysantha*	Glenwood Yellow Columbine	4	1-gal.
G	*Aquilegia elegantula*	Native Red Columbine	2	1-gal.
H	*Brunnera macrophyla*, p. 157 XPG	False Forget-Me-Not	4	1-gal.
I	*Campanula glomerata* 'Superba'	Clustered Bellflower	6	1-gal.
J	*Campanula porscharskyana*, p. 161 XPG	Serbian Bellflower	12	1-gal.
K	*Campanula rotundifolia*, p. 92 XPG	Harebell	3	1-gal.
L	*Coreopsis verticillata* 'Moonbeam'	Thread-leaf Coreopsis	4	1-gal.
M	*Dianthus deltoides* 'Crimson'	Maiden Pink	8	1-gal.
N	*Dicentra eximia*	Bleeding Heart	8	1-gal.
O	*Geranium dalmaticum*	Dalmation Cranesbill	3	Flat-32
P	*Heuchera sanguinea*, p. 163 XPG	Red Coralbells	8	1-gal.
Q	*Heuchera* 'Bressingham Hybrid'	Coral Bells (mixed)	6	1-gal.
R	*Leucanthemum* 'Aglaya'	Aglaya Shasta Daisy	8	1-gal.
S	*Lilium* 'Lemon Pixie'	Yellow Lily	3	1-gal.
T	*Mahonia repens*, p. 165 XPG	Creeping Colorado Holly	10	1-gal.
U	*Papaver nudicale*	Iceland Poppy	8	1-gal.
V	*Phlox subulata* 'Blue Emerald'	Blue Emerald Phlox	4	1-gal.
W	*Potentilla atrosanguinea*	Red Potentilla	4	1-gal.
X	*Pulsatilla vulgaris* 'Heller Hybrids,' p. 111 XPG	European Pasque Flower	6	1-gal.
Y	*Salvia argentea*	Silver Sage	3	1-gal.
Z	*Veronica austriaca* 'Crater Lake Blue'	Crater Lake Blue Veronica	5	1-gal.

Alchemilla mollis—Lady's Mantle

Rosaceae—Rose Family
Herbaceous Perennial
Height: 12 to 18 inches • Spread: 12 to 15 inches

MAXIMUM ELEVATION: 7,000 feet.

WATER: **EXPOSURE:**

FORM: Broad mound of large, scalloped leaves, sprinkled with chartreuse open-flower clusters.

LANDSCAPE USE: Excellent as a ground cover under lightly branched shrubs, appropriate for perennial flower garden.

PAGE REFERENCE: 156.

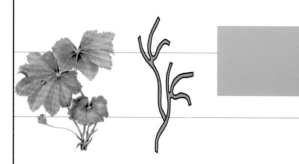

Bergenia cordifolia—Heartleaf Bergenia, Heartleaf Saxifrage

Saxifragaceae—Saxifrage Family
Herbaceous Perennial
Height: 12 inches • Spread: 12 to 15 inches

MAXIMUM ELEVATION: 8,000 feet.

WATER: **EXPOSURE:**

FORM: Wide, rounded mound.

LANDSCAPE USE: Mass grouping as ground cover, perennial flower garden.

PAGE REFERENCE: 158.

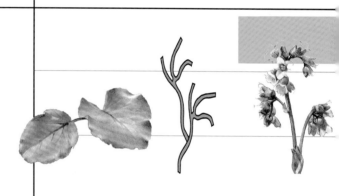

Brunnera macrophylla— Perennial Forget-me-not, Siberian Bugloss

Boraginaceae—Borage Family
Herbaceous Perennial
Height: 18 to 24 inches • Spread: 12 to 18 inches

MAXIMUM ELEVATION: 9,000 feet.

WATER: **EXPOSURE:**

FORM: Strong clumps of large, basal leaves, above which hover tiny, bright blue flowers.

LANDSCAPE USE: Partly shaded areas of the garden under open trees or among shrubs. Effective as a ground cover, specimen or in a border.

PAGE REFERENCE: 159.

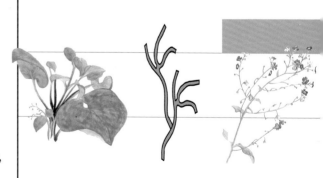

Calamintha grandiflora—Beautiful Mint
Lamiaceae—Mint Family
Herbaceous Perennial
Height: 12 to 24 inches • Spread: 10 to 15 inches

MAXIMUM ELEVATION: 6,000 feet.

WATER: **EXPOSURE:**

FORM: Erect, bushy.

LANDSCAPE USE: For the front of the border in lightly shaded areas or in containers.

PAGE REFERENCE: 160.

Campanula portenshlagiana— Dalmation Bellflower
Campanulaceae—Bellflower Family
Herbaceous Perennial
Height: 5 to 10 inches • Spread: 12 to 15 inches

MAXIMUM ELEVATION: 9,000 feet.

WATER: **EXPOSURE:**

FORM: Spreading, low mound.

LANDSCAPE USE: Rock gardens, front of the border, containers, ground cover between shrubs or other plants.

PAGE REFERENCE: 161.

Galium odoratum—Sweet Woodruff, Bedstraw
Rubiaceae—Madder Family
Herbaceous Perennial
Height: 6 to 8 inches • Spread: 15 inches or more, rhizomatous

MAXIMUM ELEVATION: 8,500 feet.

WATER: **EXPOSURE:**

FORM: Low growing spreader with erect stems.

LANDSCAPE USE: Mass grouping as ground cover, herb.

PAGE REFERENCE: 162.

Heuchera sanguinea—Coralbells, Alum Root

Saxifragaceae—Saxifrage Family
Herbaceous Perennial
Height: 12 to 18 inches • Spread: 12 to 15 inches

MAXIMUM ELEVATION: 9,000 feet.

WATER: **EXPOSURE:**

FORM: Dense clump of scalloped foliage topped with airy spikes of nodding flowers.

LANDSCAPE USE: Mass grouping as a tall ground cover, perennial flower garden, along garden path, or in the dappled shade of a tree.

PAGE REFERENCE: 163.

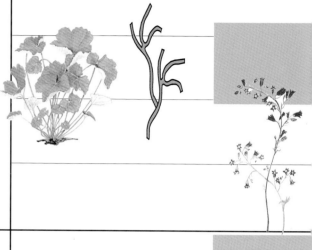

Lamium maculatum—Spotted Dead Nettle

Lamiaceae—Mint Family
Herbaceous Perennial
Height: 8 to 12 inches • Spread: 24 inches

MAXIMUM ELEVATION: 7,500 feet.

WATER: **EXPOSURE:**

FORM: Dense foliage forms on slender, spreading stems to produce a dense mat.

LANDSCAPE USE: Under trees or on the north side of structure. In borders, hanging baskets or as a tall ground cover.

PAGE REFERENCE: 164.

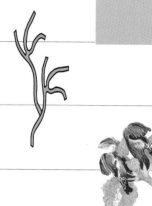

Mahonia repens—Creeping Grape Holly

Berberidaceae—Barberry Family
Broadleaf Evergreen Ground Cover
Height: 1 to 2 feet • Spread: 6 feet

MAXIMUM ELEVATION: 9,000 feet.

WATER: **EXPOSURE:**

FORM: Low spreading, coarse-textured.

LANDSCAPE USE: Ground cover under shade trees, rock gardens.

PAGE REFERENCE: 165.

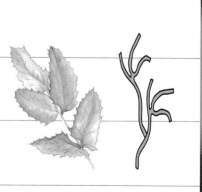

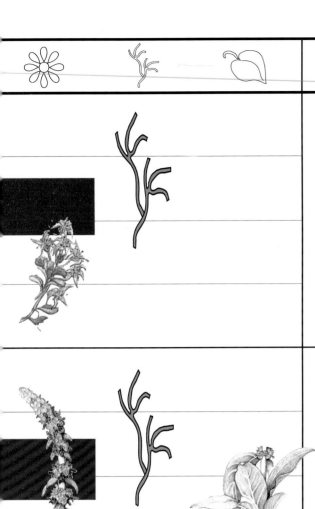

Sedum spurium—Two-row Stonecrop

Crassulaceae—Stonecrop Family
Evergreen Succulent
Height: 3 to 6 inches • Spread: 12 to 24 inches

MAXIMUM ELEVATION: 6,500 feet.

WATER: **EXPOSURE:**

FORM: Creeping succulent mat.

LANDSCAPE USE: Colorful mat throughout the seasons, providing flower and leaf color to rock gardens, path edges, and overlapping, terraced slopes.

PAGE REFERENCE: 174.

Stachys lanata (S. byzantina)—Lamb's Ear

Lamiaceae—Mint Family
Herbaceous Perennial
Height: 1 to 1½ feet • Spread: 1 to 3 feet

MAXIMUM ELEVATION: 8,000 feet.

WATER: **EXPOSURE:**

FORM: Erect flower stalks rise above low-spreading foliage rosettes.

LANDSCAPE USE: Plant as a contrast to green foliage or to set off brilliant colors in borders or perennial beds. Plant as a ground cover.

PAGE REFERENCE: 175.